THE OTHER AM

White Working-Clas
on Race, Identity, a

Harris Beider and Kusmir... ...nahal

P

First published in Great Britain in 2020 by

Policy Press
University of Bristol
1-9 Old Park Hill
Bristol
BS2 8BB
UK
t: +44 (0)117 954 5940
pp-info@bristol.ac.uk
www.policypress.co.uk

British Library Cataloguing in Publication Data
A catalogue record for this book is available from the British Library

ISBN 978-1-4473-3705-8 hardback
ISBN 978-1-4473-3706-5 paperback
ISBN 978-1-4473-3707-2 ePdf
ISBN 978-1-4473-3708-9 ePub

Cover design by Andrew Corbett
Front cover image: Prizmu, Kraków, Poland; Contributor: Richard1 / Stockimo / Alamy Stock Photo
Printed and bound in Great Britain by CPI Group (UK) Ltd, Croydon, CR0 4YY.
Policy Press uses environmentally responsible print partners

MIX
Paper from responsible sources
FSC www.fsc.org FSC® C013604

Contents

Acknowledgments

To arrive at a position where we are writing to offer gratitude to and to recognize so many people who made such a project possible is heartfelt. This project began long before we arrived in the US. It began with our own lived experiences and led us to take a journey 'across the pond'. We are grateful to all the people who shared their space, time, homes, community centres, offices to talk with us openly and honestly about their lived experiences and the challenges they saw as important. We were welcomed and supported by many people, who often went out of their way to ensure we had access to individuals and communities, including chaperoning us to meetings, introducing us to the people and organisations who make such a project possible.

We are so grateful to all at Bristol University Press/Policy Press, particularly Victoria Pittman, Shannon Kneis and Bahar Celik Muller, and Jo Morton, editorial project manager, for recognising the worth of the research and working with us to make the book possible. Thank you also to Dr Aftab Gujral for proofreading, being interested in the book and offering encouragement. Anonymous reviewers are crucial to the process, offering their expertise and insight that contributes to the whole, and we would like to thank them for the time and energy they gave to read and comment on our book.

The ideas and research data used in this book first appeared in the report *The Other America: White-Working Class Views on Belonging, Change, Identity, and Immigration*, commissioned by Open Society Foundations US Programs, and has been granted permission for use in this publication by Coventry University. We thank colleagues at the Foundation for recognizing the importance of the research and offering guidance.

Finally, we were away from home for long periods, and travelled extensively in the US. We want to thank our partners, Sarah and Corinne, who forever support, encourage and inspire us.

1

Introduction

Context

This book offers an insight into the views and experiences of white working-class communities during and following the election of Donald Trump as US President in November 2016. It further seeks to explore critically academic and policy interest in the US in and to expand on our continuing research on white working-class communities (Open Society Foundations, 2014; Beider, 2015; Beider et al, 2017). The national narrative appears to credit (or blame) white working-class mobilization across the country, and especially in the "Rust Belt" states of Michigan, Ohio, and Pennsylvania that proved to be pivotal to the success of Trump. Those who take this position see the white working class as being problematic in different ways: grounded in norms and behaviors that seem out of step with mainstream society; at odds with the reality of increased ethnic diversity across the country and especially in cities; blaming others for their economic plight; and disengaged from politics (see, for example, Bonikowski, 2016; Gest, 2016). In this scenario, white working-class communities are rooted in a past America, speaking nostalgically about a mythical nation that has long disappeared, if it ever existed, rather than the multiracial and multi-ethnic future that is likely to shape the century. Yet, while the conventional narrative about Trump, and his relation to what has become known as the "white working class," has the benefit of being presented as a straightforward connection to a forgotten majority, the experiences and conversations collected in this book offer more nuanced and challenging findings about the other America.

The rise of Donald Trump and the association with the white working class needs to be placed in the wider context of a surge in support for populism in many parts of the world. In some respects, Trump does appear to fit the definition of a populist, which has been framed as pitting a corrupt and self-serving elite against a virtuous and moral public (Mudde, 2007). Furthermore, the right-wing populism seen recently in the UK 2016 referendum to leave the European Union (EU) (known as "Brexit") and the electoral success of the Front National (FN) in France and the Alternative für Deutschland (AfD) in

Germany, along with the election of right-wing populist governments in Poland and Hungary, can also be viewed as defending the virtuous public composed of phenotypically and culturally homogeneous groups against an influx of people who are different—typically immigrants, refugees, and communities of color (Greven, 2016). Populists lend support to the "clash of civilizations" thesis put forward by Huntington (1997), based on the inevitable conflict between Christian and Muslim values, albeit that this is amplified much more in Europe in the wake of the 2015 refugee crisis and prospect of Turkey joining the EU than in the US, where the threat is arguably couched in terms of security. Specifically, within right-wing populism, the homogeneous group is composed of white working-class communities who view themselves as disconnected from the elites and under siege from economic and cultural insecurity. This is summarized by Bonikowski (2016: 11): "In recent cases of right-wing populism, such as the Trump campaign and European anti-immigrant movements, appeals to 'the people' have primarily targeted white, native-born voters, by tapping into their grievances with demographic and cultural change, as well as their dissatisfaction with mainstream politics."

Rather than viewing Trump as being isolated to the US, the evidence suggests that he is part of a global politics that has seen an upsurge of interest and now growing electoral success. As Gridron and Bonikowski (2014) state, there are many different varieties of populism: that typified by the extreme right in France, Germany, Sweden, Poland, and Italy; a nationalism couched in terms of taking on the elites, as seen in the UK and recently with Trump in the US; and a much more leftist and inclusive approach, such as in Bolivia and Brazil during the 2000s, Greece and Spain in the 2010s, and opposition political leaders such as Bernie Sanders in the US and Jeremy Corbyn in the UK. In each case, populists put forward the view that: politics (and, by inference, democracy) is broken; elites in the media, the political class, and business have become self-serving; and people have become disconnected from those who seek to govern.

The rise of Trumpian populist politics should not be seen as a novel case in the US. There are numerous examples of populist-type campaigns. For example, in the late 19th century, the Populist Party emerged with a platform to bring together rural communities who felt disenfranchised by rapid industrialization alongside civic reform. In a different way, the rise of the New Left during the 1960s, based on mobilizing young people, unions, and communities of color, could be seen as a reaction to the end of the post-1945 economic boom, allied to increased divisions in society along the line of race and class (Kazin,

1995). Donald Trump's success in 2016 may have appeared as a shock to the US political system but populist presidential campaigns—based on the elite versus the people—show more continuity than we would believe, stretching back to Andrew Jackson (1830s) and more recently including George Wallace (1960s), George McGovern (1970s), and Ronald Reagan (1980s) (Bonikowski, 2016; Galston, 2017). Therefore, populist politics is not new; however, what is new is non-political actors reaching power and challenging an established status quo.

Our rationale

The rationale of the book is to focus on how white working-class Americans view race, change, and immigration. It was a coincidence that the fieldwork took place during the primaries and presidential election, and that Trump became a major focal point of discussions. The overarching narrative on Trump's variety of populist politics is that he was supported in large numbers by white working-class communities. This group has been weaponized by the media as Trump's praetorian guard, being eager to engage with rhetoric overflowing with the demonization of immigrants, Muslims, and Mexicans, as well as bringing back jobs to working-class communities (*The Atlantic*, 2018). Trump positioned himself as the candidate for workers rather than the elite, with "working class" and "workers" among the top three terms mentioned in his 2016 campaign speeches. It is clear that he wanted to galvanize support from this group, as the following speech shows:

> It's going to be a victory for the people, a victory for the wage-earner, the factory worker. Remember this, a big, big victory for the factory worker. They haven't had those victories for a long time. A victory for every citizen and for all of the people whose voices have not been heard for many, many years. They're going to be heard again. (Lamont et al, 2017: 164)

This book takes a different perspective on white working-class communities by critically analyzing their views from a grassroots perspective. In our research, we did not have any preconceptions about the people we met in terms of their views on race, politics, and change. The methodological approach (see Chapter 2) deployed across the five case-study sites, which engaged with 415 people, was consistent and enabled participants to respond to overarching narratives on the 2016 election and support for Trump, to discuss the way in which commentators and academics have defined white working-class communities, and to identify how working-class communities at the ground level can come together to form meaningful cross-racial coalitions.

By presenting white working-class views through the lens of their lived experiences, we provide a bulwark against those who seek to construct them as a problematic other. The 2016 US election campaign weaponized the term "white working class," which became a vessel to describe people who were seen to be "deplorable," as Hillary Clinton appeared to define them during the presidential campaign: "You could put half of Trump's supporters into what I call the basket of deplorables. Right? The racist, sexist, homophobic, xenophobic, Islamophobic—you name it. And unfortunately, there are people like that. And he has lifted them up" (CBS, 2016).

The inference was that white working-class communities had been consigned as an embarrassing section of the population and were not worth engaging with or considering in the electoral or political calculus. However, this has not always been the case. A realistic view would be that the analysis of white working-class communities has seen occasional loud bangs in a continuum of deafening silence. The latter could be explained by the normalcy of being white in the US. As Richard Dyer puts forward in his classic analysis of whiteness and white privilege, the absence of these terms in research culture and general commentary is because white is taken as the norm and others—in terms of race, gender, disability, and sexual orientation—are seen as being different. This normalcy becomes dominant because of the power and dominance that white privilege has accumulated through racism and control (Dyer, 1997). Given its normalcy and ubiquity, why should commentators discuss white working-class people when compared to the pressing challenges and problems that communities of color have to confront in the everyday? In this context, it is not surprising that long silences provide the background to the discussion of white working-class people, which are punctuated by loud bangs such as the 2016 campaign. It could be argued that the Democrats, media commentators, and the research community made the mistake of viewing the white working class through the prism of problematic Trump supporters. This was a top-down framing by the policy and research elite. In short, they did not see them as being worthy of debate and discussion, writing them off as a problematic and socially constructed other. They were the invisible white norm against the visible minority. Yet, their class position and their explicit social construction as "deplorable" helped them to become visible and "weaponized" during the 2016 campaign.

The case will be made in this book that the white working class are neither a homogeneous nor an invisible group. As we will discuss in our analysis of the data, they revealed a number of different perspectives on politics, race, and change, and can be considered to be as diverse as any other community. We wanted to use the data and evidence from our fieldwork to challenge some of the overarching rhetoric and narrative framed around this group, for example: reflecting on the importance of values in shaping white working-class identity; deconstructing the view of white working-class communities as being unstinting Trump supporters, with all that implied in the 2016 campaign; and discussing the way in which, from their perspective, privilege is applied differently to white working-class communities compared to communities of color, for example, in the job market ("reverse discrimination" in favor of minorities) and in the competition for votes (with Democrats, in particular, seen as much more interested in courting minority groups and young people), as opposed to the criminal justice and policing domains (where minority groups are treated unfairly compared to white people).

The specter of rising global populism generally, and specifically the rise of Donald Trump in 2016 to become President of the US, framed our work. Our contribution shows that the lived experiences of white working-class communities complicate the conventional view of the constituency as driving populism, or being the reason for the success of Trump. It also challenges widely accepted definitions of the white working class and the lack of appetite among this group to work alongside others to form cross-racial coalitions of interest on the ground. In revealing these insights, we provide opportunities for policymakers to reconsider how white working-class communities are perceived, and how they can be engaged in a positive and inclusive way going forward.

Reviewing trends in the study of white working-class communities

This book takes a different path to our understanding of white working-class communities but nevertheless builds on an interdisciplinary literature on this group in the US, which helps to provide a context for the study. We will discuss this literature in the following, including: analyses of the integration of migrants who came to the US in the 19th and 20th centuries from countries such as Ireland, Italy, and

Germany in Europe; ethnographies in cities and neighborhoods that provide accounts of social life lived through the prism of a white lens; and more anecdotal commentary populated by media and think-tank contributions regarding national voting patterns between the main political parties.

There have been a number of contributions that examine the exclusion of ethnic white immigrants arriving in the US during the late 19th and early 20th centuries (Jacobson, 1998; Roediger, 2005). The claim from those who work in this area, known as "whiteness studies," is that the integration of white immigrants into the US may provide a pathway for the inclusion for visible minority groups. Thus, Irish, Italian, and Jewish immigrants encountered racial discrimination but, following a period of acculturation, became accepted into the white mainstream. However, comparing the integration of white immigrants with the integration of immigrants of color is not helpful because the lived experiences of the groups are different. The reality of racist violence, forced migration, and legal restrictions placed on immigrants and communities of color was markedly different in scale, depth, and longevity vis-à-vis white immigrants (see Fox and Guglielmo, 2012).

There have been several ethnographic studies about white working-class communities living in large cities, including Rieder's (1985) *Canarsie*, which shows how a low- and middle-income Italian and Jewish area of Brooklyn resisted attempts at racial integration during the 1970s. As such, some of the discussion by Rieder is similar to our own research, which shows that racialized language continues to be used in Brooklyn three decades on. Similarly, Hartigan's (1999) study of three neighborhoods in Detroit demonstrated the complexity of white privilege when applied to white residents with different types of jobs and income. Rather than viewing whiteness as being symbolically opposed to black "otherness," Hartigan observed a diversity within white working-class communities that appeared to show different types of friendships with communities of color depending on economic position. This again supports the findings from our own work on the complexity of identities and relationships in white working-class communities.

Kefalas's (2003) *Working-class Heroes* is an ethnographic study in Chicago. It showed how issues of race and class become key markers used to defend the neighborhood from outsiders. In a different vein, Linkon and Russo's (2002) *Steeltown U.S.A.* frames the impact of deindustrialization, loss, and collective memory in the context of a steel factory's closure. Monica McDermott's (2006) *Working-class White* is an account of interracial interactions in Boston and Atlanta, as seen by a participant-observer in a convenience store. The lived experience of working-class white people appears to shift from being friendly and supportive in the presence of black people to hostility in their absence.

Finally, Hochschild's (2016) *Strangers in their Own Land* and Cramer's (2016) *The Politics of Resentment* are based on ethnographic conversations in Louisiana and Wisconsin, respectively, trying to understand through deep listening how white people felt about politics, government, identities, representation, and liberal elites in their land. Their findings bring to the surface: a deep resentment toward people in society who "unfairly" benefit from government policy; anxieties of not benefiting from or being represented by a liberal urban political elite; and feelings of being ignored and often silent, or disconnected from people racially different to them who are in similar economic hardship.

There have been several recent interventions on the theme of the white working class by individuals who have partly used personal narratives to frame their analysis and description. Vance's (2016) memoir *Hillbilly Elegy* received significant publicity for telling the story of a problematic upbringing by poor white Appalachian parents who moved to Ohio in search of work. Documenting white working-class communities as being scarred by drugs, violence, and family dysfunction, Vance's portrait is not especially flattering and appears to pathologize this group. Yet, it has become celebrated given that it provided a backdrop to the rise of Trump, and is neatly summarized by *The Guardian*:

> It dropped into a national shouting match that has pitted a hazily defined entity called "the white working class" against an equally hazy "coastal elite" as the Sunni and Shia of the American political scene. The commentariat were at a loss as to explain the ballooning support for Trump, a candidate so transparently unqualified for the job that his candidacy seemed more like a prank than a serious bid for the White House. Vance, articulate and authentically Appalachian, became a regular face on the cable news circuit, a sort of ethnographic native informant about the "another America." (Kunzru, 2016)

There have been other contributions that have transcended academic and public discussion. For example, *White Trash* by Isenberg (2016) disrupts the view that class has been silent and unimportant in American history. On the contrary, poor white people were looked at in disdain by other citizens, who marked them as being problematic and ascribed pathologies to them. Williams (2017) points to the problems of reducing the white working class in terms of income and occupation, instead pointing to the "missing middle class" as the epitome of the white working class. In *What's the Matter with Kansas?*, Frank (2004) discusses reasons why the white working class has become more conservative and voted for the Republicans rather than the Democrats, and Walsh (2014) attempts to discover whether the white working class has been lost by the Democrats because of the rise of cultural politics and the move to win over the middle class.

Another element in all of these studies is how white Americans, and not just the white working class, are responding to the numerical changes occurring in the US, and how this is understood with reference both to the rise of Donald Trump and as "a challenge to the absoluteness of whites' dominance" (Jardina, 2019: 3). Jardina offers an important lens into the group dynamics of white identity and how it has emerged by coming together and coalescing as a racial group that was often invisible, the norm, and dominant but now sees that norm and dominance being challenged. The invisible has become a visible white identity political movement, as embodied by the current President of the US. The longer-term consequence of this form of bonding capital (Putnam, 2000) is a reassertion of a racial order that protects white group interests and maintains their privileged group position at the top (Jardina, 2019: 4–5).

A body of work reflecting on the political behavior of white working-class voters has been led by the policy community and think tanks. Consideration has been given to whether the white working class remains an important electoral demographic when it is shrinking as a population group, even as the US becomes increasingly ethnically diverse, college-educated, and urban. Contributions have been made by Greenberg (2014), Levison (2013), and Teixeira and Abramowitz (2008), who have, to a greater or lesser extent, warned Democrats not to take white working-class voters for granted. The most recent political analysis was undertaken by the Public Research Religion Institute (PRRI), and *The Atlantic* (2018) pointed to cultural insecurity alongside the allure of a disruptive candidate as key reasons for white working-class voters turning to Trump.

Since the rise of Trump in 2016, it seems that a new industry has been created to understand why the white working class acted in this way and against their economic interests, with articles and op-ed pieces appearing regularly in such publications such as the *New York Times*, the *Washington Post*, and *The Economist*. The narrative seems to be clear: Trump was the insurgent candidate against the political and media elite. He tapped into cultural and economic insecurity across white working-class America. The argument is clear but when scrutinized, it breaks down because the white working class is not uniform in allegiance (PRRI, 2017).

This book frames the white working class not as a singular group, but as composed of different subsections who articulate a set of lived common values. Driven by a qualitative methodology and offering a platform for people to speak about their lived experiences, our research aims to bring to the fore perspectives that challenge the conventional and often top-down framing of white working-class communities. They become multidimensional rather than the angry and pathologized precariat that is often presented by the elites operating in politics, the media, and academia. The reality is much more complex, nuanced, and context-specific compared to the "common-sense" formulations of white working-class people.

Chapter outline

Chapter 2, "Researching white working-class communities," discusses the researchers' positionality in relation to the research and the research participants. This is an area of research that is sometimes poorly represented and responded to but often important in framing the position of the researchers in relation to the researched. The chapter also details the methodological approach that led the research team to engage and interview 415 people across five cities. As a team, we were all committed to working in partnership with local activists, stakeholders, and residents wherever that was possible and appropriate.

In Chapter 3, "The lived experience of being white and working class," we argue that definitions of the white working class, which have been used extensively, need to be reconsidered. Typically, these definitions focus on non-Hispanic white people without a college degree. Yet, using this definition, the billionaire Internet entrepreneurs Bill Gates of Microsoft and Mark Zuckerberg of Facebook would be framed as members of the white working class. Clearly, this is not the case. Missing in the discussion on definition is how people themselves consider working-class life and social mores, and especially the importance of values and norms in shaping their lived experiences. We explore further the challenges of ascribing privilege to the white working-class communities who took part in our study. In our various discussions, "white" was often viewed uncritically and implicitly, and was dropped quickly, when exploring the lived experiences of the white working class by the research participants. The importance of working hard and being honest was emphasized, as well as the relevance of class. White working-class communities were viewed as classed while communities of color were often raced.

Chapter 4, "Hope and change: choosing a president," emphasizes how the rise of Donald Trump, from an outside candidate for the Republican nomination to being elected president in 2016, created a backdrop for the book. His was the "hope and change" candidacy and he clearly "weaponized" the discussion on white working-class communities by portraying himself as the victim of political elites who had no interest in the lives of ordinary people. This was in contrast to Trump's defeated opponent Hillary Clinton, who could not move from being seen as an establishment candidate who was out of touch with white working-class values, which were so important in defining who belonged to this group. The chapter takes a critical view of the white working class being positioned as enthusiastic cheerleaders for Trump.

Chapter 5, "Talking about race, identity, and change," provides the reader with an edited transcript of a focus group discussion in Phoenix, Arizona, soon after the inauguration of President Trump. It highlights the views and opinions held by the participants, which became key themes emerging from the research. More importantly, it shows a group of white residents talking about their new President, his immediate actions, and the turmoil that these actions unleashed in the US soon after he was elected.

Chapter 6, "The challenges of cross-racial coalition building," looks forward to the possibilities of building cross-racial coalitions between the white working class and communities of color as the country transitions from majority white to minority white. This will be challenging as relatively few examples were found of meaningful coalitions of interest and experiences of hard-wired diversity beyond brief encounters in public and informal spaces.

The final chapter will call for a radical overhaul of the way in which white working-class communities are discussed, engaged with, and represented by policymakers and political organizations as we look ahead to the next political cycle of 2020 and beyond. Returning to the context of rising populism across the globe, white working-class communities cannot simply be ignored. Rather the white working class should be considered to be as diverse as any other group, an important legacy population, and a community that has a range of views shaped by location, politics, and culture. This opens up the prospect of exciting possibilities for research, policy, practice, and coalition building as we move into an uncertain populist future.

2

Researching white working-class communities

Coming to America

Making a decision to undertake qualitative research in the US with white working-class communities was challenging, sometimes daunting, and often unpredictable. As researchers of long standing in the UK, we have undertaken various studies and community engagement projects focusing on race, class, community engagement, and disadvantage. Much of this research had included working directly with white working-class people in the UK or indirectly, for example, when working on the experiences of racist violence in black and minority ethnic communities. We have had a long history of working together on projects and making sense of our own experiences of growing up since the 1960s in an emerging multiracial, multi-ethnic and multicultural UK.

Our parents immigrated from India and Pakistan to the UK and settled in and near the West Midlands of England. One of us was born in the UK and the other was but a few years old when he arrived in England. We were part of the first generation of South Asian children growing up in the UK from the "mass immigration" that started in 1948 with the arrival of West Indians on the Windrush through to the early 1970s, when draconian immigration legislation slowed the pace of immigration. We had similar educational experiences in largely white schools, often only being taught by all-white teachers through primary, secondary, and tertiary education. Indeed, one of us did not meet an educator of color until postgraduate level. We both shared experiences of racist harassment and abuse in our schools at the hands of white, often male, working-class students. Yet, we also had strong multiracial and multiclass friendships. One of us grew up in a predominately white community and having white friends was considered normal. There were not always known boundaries to cross; sometimes, just having the courage to ask if one could join in to play together would build friendships.

The disjuncture between experiencing racist abuse in school by some white children and the friendships offered by other white young people was a lasting legacy for both of us. It offered us an early proto-sociological and political lens to explore the nuances of everyday life. Our experiences taught us to learn to suspend judgments about others, to be aware of the range and scope of opinions, and to simply recognize that while prejudices are rampant, not all prejudices are racist and even the "racists" can often turn the other cheek and be supportive. While situated in a particular socio-historical context, these experiences have influenced our lives, personal choices, and work. More importantly, we believe, awareness of our experiences enabled us to successfully enter the research field in the US at a pivotal point in its history as British-Indian and British-Pakistani researchers, and to closely work with and connect to the lives of white working-class people in five cities.

Our professional work has focused on community relations, with much of it on race relations. We recently came together to work on a study based in London for the Open Society Foundations (OSF, 2014) that focused on the experiences of low-income white and Muslim communities living in a multiracial, multicultural global city that is, in itself, changing through migration. This built on empirical work completed earlier (Beider, 2015) that explored how white working-class people in the UK are positioned as reactionary and racist but also focused on their lived experience of everyday multiracial Britain.

Sometimes, research becomes possible through being in the right place at the right time. We were both fortunate to be working in the US at Columbia University and Arizona State University in 2016. Having completed the OSF (2014) study in London, there was an opportunity to explore how such a study might be undertaken in the US, focusing solely on white working-class communities.

Beider's proximity to the OSF in New York contributed greatly to conversations, building interest and trust, and demonstrating expertise to colleagues at the OSF. Coupled with links with a colleague at a US university, and with Chahal situated in Phoenix, Arizona, and building links with academics and not-for profits focusing on hate crime, equality, and diversity, we felt that we had a good coverage of the US to undertake a multi-sited study focusing on the experiences of being white and working class in multiracial America.

Coming to America in 2016, we were thrown into an election campaign that, given the two protagonists, everyone had a view on. These views were emotional, vitriolic, passionate, and sometimes directly in our face. However, they were always honest and heartfelt, and cut across despair and hope.

Considering positionality

As two UK-based non-white, male researchers moving into potentially all-white spaces to undertake qualitative research, we both reflected on our perceived and actual identities and assumptions prior to, entering, and during the fieldwork:

- Would we be accepted as insiders given our obvious racial and national outsider identities?
- What fears did we have?
- How might our positionality affect, maybe even hinder, gaining access and building rapport and trust in our interactions?
- How would we deal with and be affected by racially charged language if it occurred?

There is a dearth of literature on the positionality and reflexivity of researchers when studying white working-class people. While it is not the scope of this chapter to review why this silence exists, it is pertinent to say that recent qualitative research outputs have not offered any learning from their entry into the field. This may be an expression of a perceived neutral power relation in itself, particularly if "white" people are being studied by "white" researchers. Indeed, after her extensive research in Louisiana bayou country, Hochschild (2016: 250) commented that "I think it helped that I was white, female, gray-haired, and writing a book about a divide that also troubled those that I came to know." Her perceived identities and sense of empathy with the issue under investigation, Hochschild believed, gave her a privileged access that may not be readily available to others. How would two brown-skinned, British South Asian men with beards fare in this context?

We identified studies on white working-class people that do not problematize positionality and reflexivity (for example, Gest, 2016; Kozlowski and Perkins, 2016). Other studies have shown that white working-class people have felt marginalized due to deindustrialization and a growth in non-white communities since at least the 1960s (see, for example, Marusza, 1997). We identified studies that promoted "reactionary ideas" (Maisano, 2017) about the position of the white working class, specifically the white underclass and poor (see, for example, Murray, 2012; Vance, 2016), and ethnographic accounts of how and why some white working-class people are attracted to right-wing politics (Gest, 2016; Hochschild, 2016).

→ good for other sources

Stoddart (2002) is an exception to this silence on researcher positionality and working reflexively. Recognizing that working with white participants' racism, white privilege, and whiteness could be invisible, and including herself in this, Stoddart (2002: 1262) explores her reflexive journey, aiming to mitigate against "The influence of the dominant paradigm [that] can be felt through the research process from the initial stages of developing a research question all the way through data collection and analysis."

The dominant paradigm was evident in our entry into the field. It cut across a highly charged and emotive 2016 US election campaign. Trump's speeches during 2016 were littered with references that cultivated and encouraged differences between groups: describing immigrants as a potential threat to the American people; framing the problems experienced by white working-class Americans as caused by elitist decision-making and a politically correct media and culture that ignores the needs of white Americans; and suggesting that women need protection from foreign "evil" forces (Lamont et al, 2017).

As two non-white British researchers, we recognized that Trump's speeches and rhetoric may create a febrile atmosphere, and that we would need to consider our safety and be conscious that, in some situations, conversations with white working-class people may be challenging and possibly unsafe. As such, we ensured that there were always two researchers working together in the field, and where that was not possible, that there was a local key informant working with the researcher.

Considering bias

Entering into a subject's environment requires researchers to have a reflexive awareness and approach that recognizes and adopts a position which ensures that the interactions with people, interpretations of data, and presentations of empirical material can be held up to scrutiny, are trustworthy, and are free from bias. This means having an awareness that for the research to be credible, potential for bias has to be recognized and mitigated at the outset and through the process, including through data analysis and writing up. Patton (2002: 51) suggests that this means that the researcher has to approach the study from a standpoint not of wanting to prove or offer predetermined truths, but of wanting to "understand the world as it unfolds, to be true to complexities and multiple perspectives as they emerge, and be balanced in reporting both confirmatory and disconfirming evidence with regard to any conclusions offered."

The debates on objectivity and subjectivity in the research process have often undermined qualitative research. Yet, the power to tell stories—to reflect on the lives of ordinary, often forgotten people—has a social and political resonance (see, for example, Collins, 2005; Hochschild, 2016) that equally narrates, contextualizes, and raises the levels of awareness of those impacted by the research and beyond. Qualitative research aims to be authentic, trustworthy, credible, and reflexive through the narratives it offers. Achieving a pure objective study, free of any subjective influences, is a "naive quest" (Bourke, 2014). Thus, being aware of our positionality in social research is a strategic approach that can bridge objectivity and subjectivity in qualitative inquiries. They exist in a dialectic relationship (Freire, 2000, cited in Bourke, 2014). As ethical researchers entering the field of study, we have a responsibility to reflect, recognize, and respond to our own experiences, prejudices, and social and intellectual positions, and to learn to have an empathic gaze.

Exploring empathy

Empathy is generally an ignored mode of understanding the researcher's relationship with, and toward, the researched. Patton (2002: 52) describes empathy as that which develops "From the personal contact with the people interviewed and observed … empathy involves being able to take and understand the stance, position, feelings, experiences and worldview of others." Etherington (2004) uses the analogy of running alongside a marathon runner for a few miles to give encouragement and to describe the learning experience and growth as a researcher. However, crucially, running alongside research participants builds an empathic bond regardless of the time spent with them. Running alongside enables the researcher to enter into the world of those being asked to tell us their story, and to explore with them their lives, motivations, and frustrations without our worldview interrupting their stride. Running alongside comes with an empathic responsibility and change:

> The very act of forming stories requires us to create coherence through ordering our experiences, and provides us with an opportunity for reclaiming ourselves and our histories. New selves form within us as we tell and re-tell our stories and when we write them down. When we use our own stories, or those of others, for research, we give testimony to what we have witnessed, and that testimony creates a voice. (Etherington, 2004: 9; see also Frank, 1995)

Beider (2015: 20) deliberately focused on "voices" to shift the gaze from generalized views of white working-class communities as a single, unified group with troubled identities that mark them as "other." He aimed to proffer an analysis of a stigmatized group that counterbalanced misrepresentations and negative cultural tropes defined by class and race, and to give voice to those interviewed:

> Not as being closed or resistant to change, but as eager to engage in grassroots dialogue with different communities. These voices of white working class residents challenge some of the conventional wisdom that has become embedded when we think of the interaction of these groups with the themes of immigration and social change. (Beider, 2015: 175)

When researching across differences, developing an open, empathic, and challenging research approach involves exploring our own positionality, and a reflexive view should be intrinsic to the research strategy. Stoddart (2002: 1262) suggests that this will enable the voices of those under-represented in traditional research to be heard "loud and clear." We would argue that this has to apply equally to groups that are misrepresented in research, the media, and public opinion.

Similar to Stoddart (2002), Chahal (1999) raised the issue of the silence of the processes of reflexive research and power relations that are inherent in all aspects of research inquiry from the viewpoint of a racialized researcher. Chahal (1999) highlighted how working across and within differences was fraught with tensions, and that the institutional and systemic marginalization of black and minority ethnic researchers and subjects added to this. Connecting this to our research with white working-class communities, we were mindful not to ascribe identities and worldviews to the people that we would be encountering across five cities in the US, and had this at the forefront of our research design. We debriefed regularly, raised concerns, and adapted our approach as we progressed with the research.

The research dilemma

The sociological challenge when entering difference and perceived sameness is not whether an identity or trope is held, but how it is used and how it influences people's day-to-day decision-making and everyday life. To move away from ascribed identities, we can be guided by Moerman (1974: 62) who emphasized that the "preferring of any identification should be a problematic phenomenon, not a comforting answer."

Moerman (1974) posits that the research dilemma should not be "who" a given group is, but when, how, and why the identification of that group is important. The "white working class" as a lived, analytical, and descriptive term should be explored and revealed, not accepted as fact. The study of whiteness may then get closer to similarities with other raced and classed groups, rather than the over-studied differences. Moerman argues that this may be achieved through understanding the ways in which "ethnic identification devices" are used and not adopting them as explanations. This requires the researcher to follow a reflexive approach that includes placing their own worldviews centre stage.

Exploring worldviews

To understand the voice and worldview of others, we have to understand our own worldview, and its influences, origins, and potential biases. In this sense, positionality is the social, economic, political, and historical context that informs who and where we are, and how we see ourselves and others. In social research, recognizing positionality is a process that: delineates the researcher's own position to the study; recognizes that the researcher's position may influence some or all aspects of the study; recognizes that the researcher is an intentional agent who has assumed and written from the view of being an insider; and recognizes that the researcher is able to clarify the personal experiences that have influenced the research through a reflexive approach (Qin, 2016).

In the US, there have been many sociological studies that have conceptualized whiteness (see Garner, 2009), and that have contributed to a sociology of race and racism from a sociological focus on whiteness. The "white gaze" (Yancy, 2008, cited in Garner, 2009) has been a fundamental shift away from researchers assuming whiteness as complexion to understanding what it means as a set of practices, beliefs, and ways of being (Garner, 2009).

In our study, we were concerned with similar issues but were also keen to explore how a group of people, often viewed as a unitary whole, had shared and varied views, motivations, and actions in different sites in the US. We wanted to "capture some of the messiness, contradictions and discursive associations in people's accounts of themselves" (Garner, 2009: 797) in order to bring to the fore the dynamics that unsettle an *a priori* assumption of an essentialized identity given to white working-class people. We entered the field knowing that in the US, the UK, and Europe, the "white working class" as a constructed group was seen as "the new minority" (Gest, 2016), not based on numbers, but through the perceived loss of power and position: an embattled, embittered people looking for representation and leadership in a changing, globalized context.

Research design

Qualitative research is a strategic decision that enables the researcher to enter into the real world or field of inquiry and have proximity to the people, the phenomena, and places in order to gather the lived experiences of those being researched. Fieldwork is the primary activity of qualitative inquiry, with the field representing direct and personal contact with people who are the researched in settings that are their own familiar environments (Patton, 2002: 48). Our design was exploratory (Hochschild, 2016). We wanted to be able to offer an insight into, not a definitive truth about, how people identified as the white working class experienced the world they live in across five cities in the US.

Research questions

The study (Beider et al, 2017) was guided by the following research questions:

- How do current definitions of the white working class fit with the experiences and views of this group of people?
- To what extent do national representations of the white working class as a disconnected and racist segment in American society reflect reality?
- What are the possibilities of building cross-racial coalitions between white working-class Americans and communities of color as the country transitions from majority white to minority white?

A qualitative approach

This research study focused on localized lived realities across different sites in the US, speaking to self-defined white working-class residents. By taking a case-study approach across five research sites, our aim was to generate a detailed and nuanced account of white working-class perspectives on race, identity, and change.

We were keen to explore: what it means to be white, and how white and working class are understood; views on the immediate political situation presented by the presidential election campaigns (and during the course of the research, Donald Trump's presidential victory) as a form of populism; the often-mentioned opinion that the white working class often equates with non-progressive and racist views; and opportunities for cross-racial/ethnic coalition building and alliances between diverse working-class communities. During the 12 months of the research, the political dynamics shifted dramatically in the US, and some of this has been captured by the study.

The research team developed relationships in each case-study area with organizations and individuals who acted as key informants and enablers in setting up focus groups and providing access to residents. Our approach allowed for a level of flexibility in the questions that we asked in exploring the lived experiences of residents, which gave voice to their views. We were also able to adapt to circumstances as our field-based networks increased, for example, organizing workshops with young people, spending an afternoon with a group of seniors, or talking with Uber drivers. This approach generated a depth of data and enabled the triangulation of findings from within and across the case-study sites, giving a richness to the experiences and life stories shared by all the research participants.[1]

Locations for the fieldwork

The research aimed to gather the experiences and views of white working-class people from across the US. To this end, the team selected five areas as the case-study sites: Bay Ridge, Brooklyn, New York, being a "global city"; Birmingham, Alabama, situated in the Bible Belt of the US South, and having a history as the birthplace of the civil rights movement; Dayton, Ohio, situated in the "Rust Belt," a term coined in the 1970s as the decline and closure of manufacturing industries shifted away from the North-East to the Sun Belt region in the South-West, where we selected Phoenix, Arizona; and, finally, Tacoma, Washington, in the Pacific North-West, which was selected as a city that has revitalized itself after a long period of decline since the 1960s, now being described as the most livable and walkable city in the US.

Working with civil society structures

The focus of the research that informs this book was engaging with and listening to white working-class communities about their perspectives on race, identity, and change. To do this, we engaged with civil society organizations, namely, those bodies that are part of neither the public nor private sector but occupy a space between the two, in order to gain trust, credibility, and access to white working-class residents. Of course, we note that civil society organizations have been viewed through different lenses. For example, in his classic exposition *Democracy in America*, De Tocqueville (1838) viewed civil society organizations as holding to account both politicians and the people in a still-emergent republic. In doing so, he was concerned about the "tyranny of the majority" jeopardizing ideals of equality and protections for minority perspectives. More recently, Robert Putnam's work has been influential in seeing a vibrant civil society sector as essential in supporting social capital by enabling people to participate and build reciprocity and trust within and between communities. In *Bowling alone*, Putnam (2000) suggests that the decline of civil society organizations in the US has led to a decline in trust in politics more generally. We found that both informal and formal civil society structures enabled our research by bringing local people together because they were trusted, known, and in a reciprocal relationship with these structures.

In our research, the organizations that we engaged with included foundations (Tacoma, Birmingham), small volunteer, community-led, and place-based initiatives to address specific issues in a neighborhood (Phoenix, Brooklyn), and larger funded community organizations working to deliver specific interventions and services (Dayton, Tacoma). They represented themes that both De Tocqueville and Putnam discuss in terms of attempting to bring different communities together and to build social cohesion, holding political institutions to account on the delivery of services, and having an intermediary role between government and communities. While all the organizations that we engaged with were interested in our remit and wanted to work with us on the research, they had varying levels of access to white working-class communities. The small informal civil society organizations were closer to communities and were able to mobilize participants to engage in the research. They were trusted and embedded in the communities themselves through activists living in the same neighborhood. The more formal organizations such as foundations were detached from direct work with white working-class communities. For these civil society organizations, the issue was not that they were disinterested in these communities, but rather that they did not have the knowledge or capability to engage. Networks and awareness of white working-class communities compared unfavorably with knowledge and networks of communities of color. This can partly be attributed to the policy focus and program investment addressing structural inequality, social exclusion, and racism experienced by minority ethnic communities.

Methods adopted

It was agreed with OSF that the research team would aim to hold up to 70 conversations in each case-study area. Two members of the research team supported fieldwork in each area to develop contacts and relationships, and to access residents to interview. This would give a total of 350 conversations using a variety of methods through a process of non-probability sampling. Table 1 shows that at the end of the fieldwork, the team had achieved 415 conversations using a range of approaches.

Stakeholder interviews

In total, the research team interviewed 77 stakeholders. These people were selected from a variety of sources from local state actors and non-government agencies (including a mayor, leaders of political parties, leaders of trade unions, and local newspaper editors), civic organizations (such as places of worship and community and advocacy organizations), and the business sector. We used a semi-structured questionnaire, organized around key themes and questions. Interviews lasted between 40 minutes and two hours. Each interview was recorded and fully transcribed.

Focus groups

Conversations with white working-class people in each of the five areas were achieved through organizing and inviting residents to focus groups. People self-selected as white and working class. Focus

Table 1: Methods adopted and numbers of conversations achieved

	Bay Ridge	Dayton	Birmingham	Phoenix	Tacoma	Total
Stakeholder interviews	16	17	14	18	12	**77**
Focus groups	28	27	32	27	30	**144**
Informal conversations	41	41	13	20	34	**149**
Interactive workshops	n/a	n/a	21	24	n/a	**45**
Total	**85**	**85**	**80**	**89**	**76**	**415**

Source: Adapted from Beider et al (2017)

groups were organized through key contacts that the research team had established by scouting the areas and through informal networks. "Snowball" sampling was used thereafter, using the networks and contacts of initial participants.

In total, 144 people attended one of 23 focus groups across the five sites. These focus groups were held in people's homes, front porches, gardens, and community centers, and were organized to fit participants' availability. Thus, some were held on weekends, some in the daytime, and some in the evening. Each participant was offered $20 as a "thank you" for participating. Many participants commented on how much they enjoyed the discussion, and many said that it was the first time that they had been asked for their views and that they should do this more often in their neighborhoods. Again, all interactions were recorded and fully transcribed.

Informal conversations

The research team took an innovative approach to the study; included in the methods were informal conversations with local people in public settings or "third spaces." This included bars, cafes, at work (for example, Uber drivers), local laundromats, on the streets, and at public events. The conversations were written up immediately after the interaction and provided a rich source of unstructured thoughts and opinions on the subject matter. A total of 149 interactions were recorded.

Interactive workshops

A key advantage in undertaking qualitative research is that its flexibility allows the researchers to react and adapt to changing circumstances. For example, we were given the opportunity to speak with a cohort of young people in Phoenix and Birmingham, and spent over an hour with each group.

Feedback workshops

A key part of the methodology was to return to each case-study area with interim findings that would facilitate a discussion and feed into the final report. The feedback workshops were also designed to draw out further discussions on local coalition building across class and racial groups. Half-day workshops were organized to bring decision-makers and residents together.

Data analysis

All the data were fully transcribed, coded by at least two members of the team, and analyzed using thematic analysis. This is a popular method in qualitative research and results in a rich description of the phenomena being explored that can show both patterns and differences. It is also a useful means of organizing a large amount of qualitative data, which can offer insight to the research questions.

Given the significant amount of data generated from 415 participants, thematic analysis was a useful strategy to adopt because it does not merely count numerical data and identify key words or phrases; rather, it provides meaningful patterns derived from a careful reading of and familiarization with the collected data. Thematic analysis generates initial codes that are shared and compared, identifying themes within the codes that are reviewed. The review defines and names themes and ultimately produces a report that reflects both the phenomenon and the research questions that informed the study.

The research team

The research team was made up of US and UK university-based researchers (Beider et al, 2017): two male researchers who were from the UK and were British-Pakistani and British-Indian, and a female researcher who was white American. As outsiders, we worked directly with community-based contacts to provide us with access to the communities that we interviewed and to build relationships with local people. This process built trust between the team and participants, enabled focus groups to be organized, and provided credibility to the project. The literature on outsider/insider researchers provides evidence that both positions enhance the entry and data-collection process (Kerstetter, 2012). For example, one member of the team had an insider status by virtue of being from the US and outsider status as not being from the areas where the study was based. Some research has suggested that outsiders are seen as being more objective by participants. However, other research has alluded to sameness being crucial to gaining access.

We felt accepted by participants. The length of the focus groups, the extent of the conversations, the comments made by participants that they enjoyed and/or had not talked about these issues before, and, finally, the numbers of people who came together, often in people's homes at short notice, offered us encouragement given our outside identity.

Case-study sites

New York City

Discussions took place in Brooklyn neighborhoods with strong Catholic, Italian, and Irish immigrant histories. Residents recalled tight-knit neighborhoods and looked to the future with mixed feelings of sadness and excitement. Here, the white working class has strong ties to unionized public professions in fire, police, and sanitation. Racial and ethnic diversity has always been a part of these neighborhoods; however, the growth of the Muslim population, particularly women wearing hijabs, reminds many of 9/11 and the loss of family, friends, co-workers, and neighbors who responded to the attacks on the Twin Towers. For the most part, conversations about neighborhood change were tied to immigration and national security. Although those we met here represented the most economically stable white working class of our study, they felt a sense of economic insecurity because of rising property values. Concerns about housing affordability were often overshadowed by anger toward Chinese investors who were driving gentrification and "destroying" the character of the neighborhoods. In Brooklyn, Clinton was the preferred candidate, receiving 79 per cent of votes on election day.

Dayton

Conversations took place in historically white working-class urban neighborhoods east of the Great Miami River. Residents here embrace their European immigrant and Appalachian migrant history, as well as optimism about the growing number of refugees and immigrants from Russia, the Middle East, Africa, and Latin America, who are revitalizing white working-class neighborhoods through the rehabilitation of homes, creation of gardens, and opening of new businesses. After decades of population loss and economic decline, the city is on the cusp of remaking itself as middle-class residents move back into the downtown neighborhoods. This phenomenon does cause concern for working-class residents, who have weathered difficult times, feel politically left behind, and resent the special attention given to immigrants, even though they are viewed as part of the process of revitalization. As the city undergoes this transformation, it remains hyper-segregated, with black–white tensions surfacing in conversations about neighborhood integration and safety. Although known to be a progressive area of Ohio, Montgomery County voted 48 per cent for Trump and 47 per cent for Clinton.

Phoenix

Some conversations took place in white working-class urban neighborhoods with a significant presence of Latinos and immigrants, primarily from Mexico, and others were in suburban, primarily white neighborhoods. Phoenix, Arizona, sits in the middle of some of the nation's most controversial anti-immigrant local and state legislation targeted at the undocumented population. Much of this hostility stems from the city's proximity to the US–Mexico border and decades of heavy flows of immigrants. Historically, Phoenix has had an overwhelmingly white population base. This began to change in the 1970s and Phoenix is now 65 per cent white, with the single largest ethnic category (35 per cent) being Mexican. Maricopa County, where Phoenix is situated, voted 49 per cent for Trump and 45 per cent for Clinton. Maricopa County had the highest number of votes for Trump of all counties in the US.

Birmingham

Conversations took place in working-class suburbs, where most whites live; in the city proper, 73 per cent of the population is African-American. Like Dayton, Birmingham is a segregated city with considerable racial tensions; here, they have a historical basis because of its place as a key site for the violent struggle for civil rights in the 1960s. The language expressed is less coded than in the other four sites. Birmingham, once known for the "Birmingham Steel" that built much of modern America, has endured considerable urban decline, though there has been recent redevelopment, especially in the downtown area. Additionally, religion and religious values were interspersed in many of the conversations about community life and politics, in contrast with the other case-study sites, where this was much more muted. Although our participants leaned more toward Trump, Jefferson County voted 45 per cent for Trump and 52 per cent for Clinton.

Tacoma

Discussions took place in urban and suburban white working-class neighborhoods. Tacoma was the least racially diverse city in our study, yet participants spoke with the most progressive language around diversity and immigrants. This is a striking working-class place, with the port infrastructure and warehouses forming a prominent part of the overall landscape. Residents frequently evoked the city's working-class identity with proud reference to being a cooperative community and "not Seattle," perhaps referencing the latter's association with money and elites, industry and politics. Many Tacoma residents come from outside the state of Washington and the city is considered to be the last affordable place to live on the west coast. Tacoma is quickly shedding its "Rust Belt"-like qualities as neighborhoods gentrify. Yet, white working-class neighborhoods still face many challenges related to crime, poverty, and homelessness. Surprising to many, Pierce County voted 42 per cent for Trump and 50 per cent for Clinton (a higher margin than had been expected) despite the strong union presence and being a Democratic state.

Note

1 The Coventry University Ethics Committee approved the project after a rigorous assessment. This process involved explaining the nature of the study, the methods to be deployed, how these were the best fit to answer the questions posed by the research, how research participants would be protected, and how issues of anonymity and confidentiality were to be handled, both in the collection and in the presentation of the data. We also provided the interview schedules, consent forms, and project information forms that would be given to all participants for review.

3

The lived experience of being white and working class

Introduction

This chapter focuses on the official definitions and lived experiences of being white and working class in the context of our study. Definitions on issues of class and identity are simplistic administrative frameworks that enable institutions and governments to group people together. However, definitions matter because they can shape political debates and policy responses. In this regard, the term "white working class" has been weaponized, especially in the 2016 presidential election in the US and the 2016 Brexit referendum in the UK. It has moved from being an official classification of a group of people with shared characteristics to becoming an organizing frame of reference to highlight political turbulence and the rise of populism across the world. In this chapter, we will consider how current definitions of the white working class fit with the experiences and views of this group of people. In doing so, we will state that missing in the discussion on definition is how people themselves consider working-class life and the importance they place on values and norms in shaping their lived experiences. The chapter will use data from our study project to increase our knowledge on framing white working-class communities in the US and conclude by suggesting that attempts to find a specific definition may be problematic.

Definitions of the white working class

Many of the debates in academic and policy communities have merged around using proxies of education, income, and occupation. This can be summarized in a polemic commentary that nevertheless gives a view on a settled position: "From revolutionary days through 2004 the majority of Americans fit two criteria. They were white. And they concluded their education before obtaining a four-year college degree. In that American mosaic, that vast working class was the largest piece, from the Yeoman farmer to the welder on the assembly line" (Brownstein, 2011). The basic definition of being white and working class largely rests on those who self-classify as white, are over the age of 25, and are without a four-year college degree.[1] This has been consolidated by a recent report from Opportunity America, the American Enterprise Institute, and Brookings that reflected on the working class in the US after the 2016 presidential campaign. It defined the working class as "adults between the ages of 25 and 64, with household income between the 20th percentile (around $30,435 for a house-hold containing a married couple with one child in 2016) and the 50th percentile ($69,254), with a high school degree or more, but less than a four-year college degree" (Opportunity America et al, 2018: 23). The report also suggests that the white working class accounts for 58.6 per cent of the US population (Opportunity America et al, 2018: 23). Some have suggested that the white working class is composed of non-Hispanic white people who have not completed a four-year college degree (McDermott and Samson, 2005; Teixeira and Abramovitz, 2008; PRRI, 2012, 2017; Levison, 2013). Educational achievement is used because it is a proxy for human capital, as well as a probable career trajectory. In short, college graduates are likely to earn 25 times more than high-school dropouts (Teixeira and Abramovitz, 2008: 3). Deploying education as the main criterion for measuring class in the US is also a practical tool because it enables questions to be standardized across surveys. Yet, the expansion of higher education has coincided with a turbulent national economy marked by the foreclosure crisis and the economic crash of 2007. In our study, many people were college graduates and yet their world was a collapsing middle class (Williams, 2017) and being sucked into the struggles of being working class. A college education had not resulted in the "American Dream" being realized with consequently increased social mobility. The reality was that many felt stuck at best or were going backwards in terms of disposable income and struggles to "keep their heads above water."

Apart from education, income and occupation have also been used to define the working class (Teixeira and Abramovitz, 2008; PRRI, 2012; Center for American Progress, 2017). Occupation creates a powerful imagery of the types of jobs historically associated with the working class. That is the view of workers in the "Rust Belt" in traditional blue-collar employment in car factories and steel mills who make enough of a salary to look after themselves and their families. The problem with grounding the definition in job type is that the US, like many other advanced industrial countries, has faced significant economic restructuring. There has been a considerable

v. good

decline in manufacturing jobs and a rise in the service sectors (Center for American Progress, 2017; Opportunity America et al., 2018). As Williams (2017) has noted, an occupational link to class is based on nostalgia about working-class life rather than borne out of reality.

Income has also been used to define the working class. Teixeira and Abramowitz (2008: 4) suggest that those with household incomes of less than $60,000 are working class, or if the definition is tighter, less than $30,000. However, income creates problems because people are reluctant to disclose their earnings and survey questions do not consistently ask questions on money earned per household (PRRI, 2012). In addition, income and earnings show geographical variation, which makes class comparison across the country almost impossible when looking at, say, New York City and Birmingham, two of our case-study areas. More than this, a low-income threshold means that being working class is restricted to very poor people and does not capture those who are working in higher-paid jobs but struggling "paycheck to paycheck." Most, but not all, of the very poor are not white, but immigrants and people of color.

One of the contributions of our research is to add to official definitions the nuance of the lived experiences of our research participants. In our study, graduating from college with a four-year degree did not, in itself, exclude a person from being part of the working class. Indeed, many of our respondents thought that a college education had no bearing on whether you could be considered working class or middle class. This skepticism of college education determining class position is further questioned by data which showed that a majority of white working-class people considered college education to be, on balance, more of a risk than an investment in terms of social mobility (PRRI, 2017). The data from the PRRI project points to the importance of work as a way to improve social mobility and secure the immediate interests of family. Our research also shows that work and being in employment were viewed as being an essential part of belonging to the working class. In this way, the importance of securing a job and thereby supporting your family emphasized the "working" part of being working class. Some participants in our research completed their education at high school determined to get a job, with few in their immediate networks of family and friends having experience of college. Others had gone on to college and some even had postgraduate qualifications. However, their experience, especially after the economic recession of 2008, was of low-paid and low-skilled work.

In short, the white working class represents a myriad of economic and social positions that cannot be reduced to policy definitions. Our research attempts to add lived experience to the official definitions of the white working class. This will be discussed later in the chapter and aims to shift away from the current position that defines the white working class as a more uniform stratum by race, education, and position in the labor market. People themselves spoke about different types of working class that did not fully correlate with these themes.

"White" is unspoken but implicit

Our research across the five case-study areas found that "white" in "white working class" became silent very early on in focus group discussions. "White" was rarely mentioned when participants started debating the definition of the white working class. *White* was always implicit in the conversations. In this way, we are reminded of the work of Dyer (1997), discussed in Chapter 1, who stated that the absence of whiteness in focus group discussions is because white is taken as the norm and others, defined in terms of race, gender, disability, religion, and sexual orientation, are seen as being different. In the majority of cases, the people we interviewed, and especially those who were residents, had not considered their whiteness as being a source of power and privilege. On the contrary, they were very critical of seeing their class position as being associated with access to privilege when the reality of their lived experience was reduced levels of income and lack of access to decent jobs. The following quote from Birmingham, AL, demonstrates resentment against the affirmative action policies operating in the police force that penalize white men: "*I'm still waiting for my white privilege. Can I speak about the white male situation because working in law enforcement … [w]hen women and minority, minorities, African-Americans enter the workforce in the law enforcement, white males were passed over, white males were discriminated against in promotion*" (Birmingham Focus Group [FG]). The participant overlaps racial resentment with a lack of privilege compared to minority groups.

Similarly, another participant was denied an opportunity to secure a scholarship to pay her way through college because she was white and her parents did not fall into the benchmark salary. Her story of her friend plays into racial tropes about Hispanic women who get pregnant to secure unfair advantage over white people and then abuse their fortuitous luck through reverse privilege:

> 'I remember a perfect example, applying for college, and I remember applying for some scholarships and I am sorry to

> say it but I didn't qualify first of all because (a) I'm white, (b) my mom was in a certain income bracket which really wasn't extraordinary … but a girlfriend of mine, which was Hispanic, got pregnant at senior, in high school, had her child, got a full boat ride to go to school, had so much money left over she bought a car, and didn't have to work. That was appalling to me.' (Phoenix FG)

Communities of color were racialized by white working-class residents in a number of ways, for example, from commentary about the inequities of welfare, to banal unawareness of the issue of race, all the way to an active framing of some groups as being problematic and criminal. The latter was revealed especially when people discussed issues of neighborhood change, immigration, and race.

Racist tropes and stereotypes were used by some white working-class residents in Birmingham, AL, when framing how the city has deteriorated and changed with the increase in the size of the black population and the greater political influence exercised by this group. These stretched from high levels of crime and concerns about personal safety when driving into the city, to poor standards of governance and control by local politicians and staff, to frustration at not having representation or a voice to influence the city. Birmingham is a majority black city, with 74 per cent of the population being African-American. These negative perspectives on change could be seen as a proxy for race and pathologies about black communities, whether the concerns were about fears of black masculinity and the black body (crime), or black competency and leadership (city governance).

The discussions with white working-class communities in Birmingham illustrated that whiteness was seen as implicit in the othering of communities of color. Indeed, it became evident that participants were talking about black people. In part, the view of some appeared to be that Birmingham was good when it was a majority white city and was controlled by white politicians but became bad when it became a black majority city and black politicians took up leadership positions. The transformation of political power was seen by some as manifested in the way that white people were now treated by some black people. The following quote about the experience of a participant's father highlights the problem as racism is excused: "*And they would come in with really nice cars, and not be like run down old cars…So my dad would be seen as racist, like, really racist, but I know him well enough to know that it's just because people have treated him horribly.*" (Birmingham FG)

The sentiment "I feel like a stranger in my own community" was often repeated in the case-study cities. This lamented change linked with increased levels of immigration and ethnic diversity, as well as increased competition for welfare, jobs, education, and housing. Again, the emphasis on "my community" makes an implicit assumption of whiteness and territoriality. People interviewed focused on working class rather than white when referring to communities and neighborhoods but it was clear that the nostalgia was framed to a large extent before places became diverse. Some of those interviewed, mostly those in their 70s or older, have become estranged from their neighborhoods because the white working-class infrastructure of churches, social and working men's clubs, bars and diners, and grocery stores that had hitherto provided common points of reference for white residents had been all but swept away by demographic changes (see also Putnam, 2000). For example, in Bay Ridge, some seniors complained about going into a grocery store and hearing people speaking in Arabic rather than English, or Chinese people not saying "hello" on the sidewalk as they passed. Again, whiteness is unspoken but the view being put forward is that in "my community" in a previous time, this would not have been the case.

College educated and working class

A college degree has been the cornerstone of defining class in the US. Yet, our participants questioned whether this could ever be a valid reason to label someone as working class or middle class. The following quotes suggest that the term itself is rooted in the past, or "antiquated." Going to college does not necessarily result in becoming middle class as the reality of being a graduate but with non-graduate levels of income and the consequent economic insecurity locks people into the category of working class: "*I think that the definition of working class is almost antiquated in the sense that it is today because just like … said they're college educated but they're still identified as working class and based on the figures, that they would still probably be considered working class*" (Dayton FG).

Many commentators have accepted that education has an important role in determining class position. Specifically, being working class is associated with completing education at high school while being middle class means going all the way through to college and having a degree (McDermott and Samson, 2005; Teixeira and Abramovitz, 2008; PRRI, 2012, 2017; Levison, 2013; Center for American Progress, 2017; Opportunity America et al., 2018). We are suggesting that this is only one of many different definitions and does not take into account the lived experiences of being white and working class. The following quote illustrates the complexity in defining and understanding what it means to be white and working class:

> 'And I said like I feel like I am working class. I'm college educated, I have a master's degree, I taught. Because it's not a very high income. Like, I'm almost thinking of it in terms of how, in the past, like she said I look at, she considers working class to be a blue-collar type of thing. Which would be the laborers etcetera. And to me, I said I feel like I am working class. I don't make a high salary. It's a middle income. And that, to me, is working class. I don't have lots of money. I can't buy the big house; I can't buy a yacht. You know, so I am a working-class person and I'm not a laborer. I'm not uneducated and I feel we kind of have the same view of it. And I think what everyone has said, it can have so many meanings.' (Bay Ridge FG)

The respondent "feels" working class although this is not manifested in terms of experiences in reference to college, work, or income. The participant has been to college and graduate school but this does not catapult her into being middle class according to her lived experience. The self-perception about being working class is strongly linked with low levels of income, albeit that the parameters of income are not provided. There are no indications that this is below the $52,000 threshold for defining working class, as discussed in Chapter 1. In our preceding example, the differentiation is between "*a high salary*" and "*middle income*," with working class denoting the latter rather than the former. This individual is earning a good salary but not enough to feel both comfortable and financially secure. There is a fluidity to being white and working class in contrast to the sometimes-simplistic administrative fixes assigned to the group in official discourses.

Lived experiences: occupations, economic insecurity, and inflexibility

In our study, the lived experiences and values were much more important to those we interviewed in shaping white working-class identities than a college education or levels of income and, indeed, occupation. The following explanation of what it means to be working class was provided by a woman in her 30s, a mother with three children, who had grown up in Birmingham, AL. In short, you work and you are working class:

> 'Working class, to me, is my background … my mom was an administrative assistant, worked all my life, my father was a police officer. I'm a hairstylist, just, you know, right out of high school, you know, you get out, you work. There was some college education but just, you know, you work, you go to work every day and you're working class.' (Birmingham FG)

The literature on the white working class seems to apply the definition to people who either are in receipt of welfare or have unskilled jobs in construction, factories, and laboring (see, for example, McDermott and Samson, 2005). Yet, in the preceding quote, the participant links being working class to occupations such as administrative assistant, police officer, and hairstylist, in contrast to traditional perceptions of working-class occupations. The values of going out to work and looking after your family are more important to this person than the type of occupation.

Our study shows that the white working class constitutes a multilayered lived experience covering a range of occupations, income levels, and educational experiences. The following quote is taken from a focus group convened in Phoenix, AZ:

> 'I think there are different levels of working class. I mean you have my dad, not educated, but head of department [retail], but is still working class. He is not making a significant income, but enough to get by … then there are professionals, like social workers, that are working class and making a difference in the community.' (Phoenix FG)

Here, the participant suggests different categories of working class related to employment functions. This includes those who work in retail who are part of the service industry, as well as people such as teachers, social workers, police officers, and firefighters who provide a public service. Educational qualifications are not part of the calculus determining who belongs to the working class.

The importance of service, whether by working in a shop and serving the public, or working in government and supporting and protecting the public, resonate with how people spoke about the importance of working-class values. These are about being selfless, demonstrating reciprocity, and serving the common good.

By moving away from conventional definitions of working class, participants instead wanted to place emphasis on their lived experiences of daily economic insecurities. These insecurities were expressed in relation to paying rent or mortgage payments on their homes, the fragile nature of employment and contracting, and the struggle to balance saving with the necessity of providing for their families.

The ideal of the "American Dream" has been built on rising levels of income and economic security at work and in housing (see later). The 2008 economic downturn has punctured the "American Dream" (Center for American Progress, 2017; Opportunity America et al., 2018) and people across different types of jobs and different income levels are feeling economically insecure, with stagnant growth in incomes combined with the legacy of the housing foreclosure crisis. In our study, as people described their daily struggles to maintain their living standards, there was a perception that the middle class is shrinking and the working class has expanded.

This perception of a shrinking and insecure middle class can be demonstrated by discussions held across the case-study sites, for example, in Dayton, OH. In the first of these discussions, people were mostly college educated and worked as school teachers, computer analysts, or in the media. These would be described as middle class yet they spoke at length about their lived experience of economic insecurity, such as being on fixed-term contracts. In the second focus group, all the people completed their education at high school and were employed in roofing, as van drivers, and as laborers. Typically, these were seen as working-class occupations. This group also spoke about economic insecurity and about the casualization of work. The most often quoted expression in these two focus groups and across the remaining case-study locations was "living paycheck to paycheck." Another expression used to describe the lived experience of economic insecurity was "barely making it" despite working two or more jobs. To people in our study, being working class meant limited economic flexibility: "*I am working hard enough to have the American Dream but I don't just have it. I am doing this whole living from paycheck to paycheck*" (Tacoma FG).

Living in precarious economic circumstances was a recurring and persistent theme throughout the study. There existed an immediacy of pending economic crisis if a month of normal income was lost, with the social mobility promised by the "American Dream" being upended and replaced with the lived experience of economic hardship.

The following two quotes drawn from Tacoma and Dayton show how people endured this struggle because of the necessity to look after their families:

> 'For me, it was just paycheck to paycheck because if you have kids you take care of, make sure they have clothes on their back.' (Tacoma FG)

> 'I've always kind of considered working class as if you were to miss a paycheck, you would be in serious straits, whereas middle class might be able to get away with a check or two.' (Dayton FG)

Many key informants[2] were puzzled as to how to engage actively with these communities as their focus had been on working with communities of color. A minority of key informants was actively hostile to white working-class communities and viewed them as a problematic "other" who displayed views on race and immigration that needed to be challenged. For example, in Phoenix, a key informant showed visible disdain for, as well as a level of disconnection from, white working-class people: "*I mean, I think for a really long time, I didn't associate or like want to associate with working class*" (Phoenix, Key Informant [KI]). The inference in this quote is that key informants who held this view either excluded or downplayed the white working class as being part of the policy landscape in their case-study locations:

> 'I think like, to start, working class, to me, are folks that are kind of like getting by financially, kind of like paycheck to paycheck, maybe not in the, you know, like lower levels of organizations in that way, some of the more like blue-collar work, so to speak. And I guess where I have been thinking of myself in that is that like I definitely work paycheck to paycheck. I am kind of like just about minimum wage in terms of what I make but I'm like a program manager at university.' (Phoenix KI)

Yet, even this key informant recognized that they too could be part of the working class because of meeting the key criterion of financial insecurity or, again, living "paycheck to paycheck."

The most problematic part of defining white working-class people was income thresholds (McDermott and Samson, 2005). As we have noted, while the majority of people interviewed agreed on the lived experiences of economic insecurity and inflexibility ("paycheck to paycheck") that separate the working from the middle class, there was a profound level of skepticism on the merit of an annual income ceiling of $52,000 in describing a "working-class" income. For example, our participants in New York City stated that this level of salary may result in economic hardship given the high costs of living, especially housing, but in Birmingham, AL, people considered this a high wage that created opportunities to be part of the middle class. In short, regional disparities in the costs of living make it very difficult to categorize the working class on the basis of income:

> 'I think that goes along with two-income households and still needing enough, needing both to survive in today's kind of economy and society, and I think it also depends on where you live because I don't think that $52,000 would work in Phoenix, at least in Phoenix proper, whereas that might work in some other locations in the country. So I think it's a tough kind of sell to put a number like an exact number on an income level because I think it fluctuates so much depending on where you live, how many kids you have, kind of the location … $52,000 in New York City? Good luck[!]' (Phoenix FG)

The result of "doing two or three jobs" is about trying to ensure that there is sufficient money coming into the household to pay bills and buy food and clothes. It can also lead to an adverse impact on family relations and life. Individuals wanted to be in work despite the reality of low pay and the loss of time. They felt that it was their duty to support and maintain their family even though time with children and partners was lost:

> 'We said that sometimes there's a loss of family time or time in general because you are always at work.' (Phoenix FG)

> 'I have to say as a working-class mom, like no matter what, given any situation, you know what you have to do as a responsibility, the distance that you have to go, hours you have to work. You are going to do whatever it takes. What inspires you is the family.' (Phoenix FG)

> 'I am a janitor and ride a bus [multiple buses]. Two hours to get there and two hours back.' (Phoenix FG)

An official definition of not having a college degree places a person into the category of working class. Our study showed that this measure was marginal to determining class status. People defined themselves as being part of the white working class irrespective of whether they ended their formal education at high school or college. Similarly, the other two components that defined working class—occupation and salary—were also seen to be less important in reality when speaking to people, as opposed to in official frameworks. Instead, people referenced their shared lived experiences and concerns about economic insecurity and job inflexibility as shaping working-class identity.

In the study, people had and shared diverse housing experiences. For example, some had lived in trailer parks and felt either totally cut off from the working class or at the bottom stratum. "White trash" or "trailer trash" was used by elites to frame some places in the US as backward and the term is deployed to pathologize people and places politically and in a negative way.

One of the most dismissive depictions of white working-class communities in popular discourse is the term "trailer trash" or "white trash." This evokes a degenerative group of poor white people who live on the margins of society in trailer parks or shacks and on welfare. In their attitudes and behaviors, for example, alcohol abuse, uncontrolled and ill-disciplined children, intermittent violence, and lack of care for their personal appearance, they show themselves to be out of step with societal norms.

These "common-sense" constructions of some sections of the white working class are not new to the 2016 presidential campaign. Isenberg (2016) suggests that the term dates back to British colonialism, when undesirable people from the UK were dumped in the wastelands of rural America, with the new country seen as a workhouse. Similarly, Wray (2006: 8) shows how the term endured from the 19th century because middle- and upper-class white people used it to keep a distance from poor white people, whom they viewed with "moral outrage, disgust, anger, contempt, and fear." Pruitt (2016) suggests that the existence of the term "white trash" may help to break down the monolith term "white working class" because the former only ever refers to a sub-segment of the latter, with the labeling of "dirty" and lazy" being used interchangeably to differentiate the groups.

In our study, participants recognized the negative coverage in the media about Trump and his supporters being consigned as "white trash" or "trailer trash." Some criticized the media for attempting to pathologize white working-class communities in this way when the reality was a multilayered lived experience:

> 'We have tornados you know … they go around, they destroy everything, you watch the news, they always find the guy who is out in front of his trailer that gets tore up, he has like five or six dogs running around … cars in the yard … teeth missing, cussing, but hates the people that are [on] welfare. When you interview him, he's not well spoken, that's trailer trash.' (Birmingham FG)

This type of framing resulted in the term "working class" becoming sullied. The imaginary being conjured up has problematic behaviors melded with comedic value, which is some distance from the reality of the respectful and law-abiding community that many in our study wanted to put forward.

Some evidenced this by recounting their own housing experiences, which included spells of living in a trailer when this was what they could afford, or having family and friends who currently lived in trailer parks. The high cost of housing meant that trailers were, and continue to be, an affordable form of accommodation for low-income communities. Participants stated that rather than the stereotypical image of being "dirty" and on welfare, people in trailer parks more often worked than not, and cared for their families in the same way as the rest of society. In this context, their lived experience was perceived as being part of a fluid and not a fixed working-class position:

> 'Yes, I grew up in a trailer for many years when we were in the military … I think people think about trailer trash sometimes, well, those are folks that are bums, they're the ones that don't have jobs, they've got ten kids running around and like that kind of thing.… They're the working class, so can trailer trash still be working class, absolutely they can be.' (Tacoma FG)

The views of the participants in our study show that attempting to define the working class is not straightforward. The "common-sense" imagery associated with the working class and, indeed, communities depicted by recent publications (see Vance, 2016) is of a "hillbilly" or "trailer trash": in short, someone who conforms to the poorest sections of society in receipt of welfare and/or in very low-paid work. Some people that we interviewed during the course of the study were in relatively well-paid occupations—teaching, policing, local government, and health—but were struggling to pay their regular bills and provide for their families.

The importance of values

The people who attended resident focus groups across our case-study sites all claimed that they belonged to the white working class. This was despite having incomes ranging below and above the $52,000 median ceiling and having jobs as diverse as roofer, delivery driver, school bus driver, hairdresser, teacher, computer programmer, community organizer, police officer, firefighter, university professor, and hospital doctor, as well as being unemployed. Their education ranged from stopping at high school to completing college and graduate school. This mix demonstrated that the monolithic white working class is, in fact, an eclectic mix of people. However, the common theme that cemented these fragmented groupings, who would otherwise have very little in common, was working-class values. Income and occupation may vary and change but values remain fixed and cohesive, as well as providing a framework to guide life.

In our study, there were three core emerging values that participants voiced across all case-study areas. First was the importance of hard work that earns a monetary reward and supports the family network. Finding and sustaining employment meant being independent from government and earning self-respect, as well as providing a role model for others in the family. Second was the wider responsibility of providing support to and showing reciprocity with people who live in the same neighborhood, especially when they need support if they have fallen on hard times. Many recounted how the mutual support operated in practice in terms of childcare circles, sharing a car to get children to school, and sharing income or supporting food shopping. Third was the critical issue of honesty and trust inside and outside the family. This was delivered in not claiming welfare that you were not entitled to or simply being very direct in the delivery of a message.

These values provided a code for white working-class communities to relate to each other and the world outside, and to consider who should be included in the working class. Hard work and independence were seen as key to being working class:

> 'I came from … a very working-class background and it was instilled in me that you take care of yourself. You work hard. And I do think that is working class. Like, I take care of myself, I don't ask for assistance.… I'm going to get my job; I'm going to support myself, you know, I'm not going to depend on anyone else. So, in that way, I consider that a

> value system and I think a lot of working-class people have the same thing, value system.' (Bay Ridge FG)

The notion of working hard seemed to be a torch that was being passed on through the generations. In this context, working-class people are not seeking assistance from anyone else to help with social mobility. Interestingly, this person appears to baulk at those who are on welfare and dependent on the state, as well as at those who can use family contacts to give them access to a job or college that they would not otherwise deserve. Noting that the fieldwork was undertaken during the 2016 presidential campaign, this showed the appeal of the outside candidatures of Donald Trump and Bernie Sanders: Trump because he claimed to have developed his business independently without the help of the state; and Sanders because he railed against the nepotism and self-serving nature of the rich and powerful.

The following quote from a labor organizer contrasted the gritty city of Tacoma with its neighbor, glitzy Seattle. In doing so, he framed Tacoma as a working-class place because the people make things happen rather than simply talking about issues interminably as they would do in Seattle. In short, the people of Tacoma work hard, echoing working-class values, and made things that contributed to the common good, as well as earning a wage to support themselves and their families. By referencing these values in Tacoma, he also bridges with other towns and cities across the US and demonstrates that people in different places have common values:

> 'I don't want to be Seattle. I really don't like Seattle.... I always tell people that this is a place that if you want something done, people will do it. These are the people that take all the dreams that are produced out of Seattle and actually make them a reality.... It's very similar [to] Rust Belt cities ... working-class people just trying to make a living out here.' (Tacoma KI)

In the following quote, being working class is again associated with hard work and economic inflexibility as you have to work to earn an income, you cannot afford the economic consequences of being sick, and you must be resilient: "*I consider the working class hard workers. The ones that go every day, if you're a little sick, you don't stay home*" (Dayton FG).

As we have noted, in discussions with participants, the theme of how the working class experience a lack of choice that creates an inflexible environment, for example, because of rigid work hours and having to

See Oak?

work to support themselves and their family, was one way to consider this group, though as the following key informant notes, "*that's a weird way to define working class*," perhaps recognizing that education, occupation, and income are more traditional methods. This person is emphasizing the importance of working hard and the lack of choice in the lived experience of being working class:

> 'I would say, you know, in that middle-income area, you know, not executive level. I really, it's hard to, you know, at least there's still some flexibility … they have no flexibility and that's a weird way to define working class. But these people, it is literally eight to five and there is no out, there is no flexibility, they've got to be there, they've got to have this job. You know, there is very little, if they need to take off for work or anything, they have a lot of trouble with that because they haven't reached that level in their career where they can say, "I'm going to be out a few days, I've got some things to do," and it's okay.' (Birmingham KI)

Perhaps the key informant reminds us of the daily grind of work as the lived experience of these communities. For some, there is no opt-out or flexibility in terms of hours of work or, indeed, working from home when, for example, a family member is unwell.

Moving away from the labor market, our participants emphasized the importance of attempting to give your best at all times, supporting your family and wider community, and especially being able to be relied upon in times of difficulty. Trustworthiness and dependability were an integral part of the moral code for many participants in the study, and were self-reinforcing:

> 'Working-class values? Well, you put pride in your work or your profession. You try to do a good job, you try to have good attendance, good work ethics. You know you're dependable.' (Tacoma FG)

> 'Humility, resilience, family and community, sacrificing for the next generation, hard working, paying your way.' (Phoenix FG)

> 'I think I got this from the military; you just go out and do the best job you can. You report to work early, you leave work late, and you are always there if somebody takes off a

> day at work to step in his place. You just establish yourself and build a reputation as being a guy with a great work ethic.' (Tacoma FG)

In contrast, they pointed negatively to those who cheated the welfare system to claim benefits unfairly, as the following quote shows:

> 'I went to welfare and seen somebody driving a brand new car and have brand new Jordan's, bitching about the amount of food stamps they are getting.... I said, "If you don't like what you're getting, get out of line and let me turn my paperwork in … because I need my food stamps, I am off work right now and you're bitching about what you're getting and you're driving a brand new car, wearing brand new Jordan's, brand new hat that matches a shirt, so somewhere you're getting money. I'm driving an '82 Chevy!"' (Dayton FG1)

This person from the East End of Dayton never discussed the "white" of "white working class." Closer examination of the quote shows the othering taking place of immigrants and communities of color as somehow not playing by the rules in claiming welfare. "They" cannot only be claiming welfare when they are able to drive around in new cars and buy decent clothes, the inference being that people of color are abusing the welfare system while white working-class people are disadvantaged because they play by the rules.

A key informant from Birmingham, AL, emphasized the similarities between white and black communities in a working-class city. Like Tacoma, with its industrial port and logging, the steel foundries in Birmingham created employment for people in the 19th century. The definition of working class is grounded in the type of work undertaken in these industries:

> 'From the history of Birmingham, I guess you could say a working-class demographic was more of a labor-based position as opposed to a service-based position … if you drop white from your description, I think we're hand in glove with a lot of the issues like what Dayton, Ohio, what you're going to see there or rural Oregon, that when industry declined in Birmingham in the '50s and '60s, the population, all that was left behind was the working-class population.' (Birmingham KI)

Again, similarities in place are made with Tacoma and Dayton. This participant also evokes working-class communities as "*left behind*" or forgotten by political and economic elites. This is discussed in Chapter 4 as one of the reasons why voters took to Trump and Sanders in 2016 because both candidates voiced their concerns.

Conclusion

As we have discussed elsewhere in the book, "white" was largely silent throughout the discussions with participants across all the sites. People were much more comfortable with using "working class" rather than "white working class" to describe themselves. In this way, they classed themselves and raced communities of color, and did not articulate or often comprehend that raced groups can be both people of color and working class. As Dyer (1997) suggests, white was nowhere but everywhere. It was a taken for granted and seen as a neutral identity.

The focus was very much on the "working" of "white working class," with frequent references to the importance of hard work and how this brings in an income, which allows for the person to become independent and have the ability to support the immediate family and wider community. Prioritizing work and the lived experience of insecurity opened up core values of reciprocity and trust as the glue that held different people with different incomes and levels of education together. Recognizing the way in which values are so important may enable policymakers and researchers to improve their understanding of working-class communities. Focusing on lived experiences provides a dynamic and fluid way for policymakers to better understand white working-class communities.

This chapter demonstrates the complexity of defining what it means to be white and working class in the US. In contrast to participants who spoke at length about the importance of values, this was only marginal in discussions with key informants, who defaulted to focusing on college education, blue-collar jobs, and occasionally income thresholds. However, unlike participants, key informants were much more willing to highlight the "white" part of "white working class" and to identify white privilege as a way to challenge the concerns of white working-class communities about being disconnected and left behind. This was overlooked by residents but remained implicit in discussions when situating communities of color or talking about crime.

This chapter commenced with contrasting official definitions with the lived experiences of people who identified as white and working class. The evidence demonstrated that the official account of emphasizing the importance of a college education, employment in "blue-collar" industries, and placing a ceiling threshold on income were at variance with the views of white working-class people. Instead, they spoke about economic insecurity irrespective of occupation and the lived experience of "living paycheck to paycheck." The term "working class" was articulated through a lived experience and memory that gave a set of values and identities. These included working hard, reciprocity, and honesty, and held sway across location, occupation, and income.

The implications of a recalibration of the white working class have already been played out in the 2016 presidential election and the rise of Donald Trump from an outlier candidate to his ascent to the White House. As discussed in Chapter 4, Trump and Bernie Sanders accessed the political capital of this wider white working-class grouping and the importance of working-class values in a way that was lost by their opponents. Much more work needs to be done to explore whether a nuanced approach to defining the white working class can be more meaningful. At the very least, there is a need for both policymakers and academics to rethink their understanding of white working-class communities through the lens of lived experiences.

Notes

1 It should be noted that Arab-Americans also classified as white in the US Census.

2 Largely composed of community organizers and local government officials.

4

Hope and change: choosing a president

Introduction

In many ways, it was fortuitous that the fieldwork and data collection that this book draws upon took place in 2016 and 2017. These were no ordinary years in US politics. It was in the midst of the campaign to elect the 45th president of the US that we undertook our research across five sites in Birmingham, Dayton, New York City, Phoenix, and Tacoma, interviewing a total of 415 people. Our focus on the perspectives of white working-class communities from these case-study areas on society and change coincided with the extraordinary rise of Donald Trump from a virtual "no-hoper" in the Republican primaries to being elected as US President in November 2016. This ascent and his campaign themes on the people versus the elites, identifying suspect communities (whether people of color or immigrants), and promising to keep factories and coalmines open provided key talking points throughout the fieldwork.

The Trump candidacy was about "hope and change" and running against the establishment as an outsider or non-politician. In this way, it could be put forward that the 2016 Trump campaign was similar to the 2008 Barack Obama campaign given that Obama was also an outsider taking on the Democrat establishment with a slogan of "hope and change"—and, of course, in the personage of Hillary Clinton, they faced the same opponent. However, the similarities end abruptly between the two varieties of "hope and change" because, unlike Obama, Trump was not appealing to communities of color, young people, or, indeed, voters who lived in large urban metropolitan areas. His pitch was to those left-behind communities who had been forgotten and felt ridiculed by the establishment and the elites. The conventional narrative was that this was an unashamed appeal to the white working class in which Trump "weaponized" and gave potency to the very term by portraying himself as also an outsider and victim of the establishment. He successfully portrayed his Democrat opponent, Hillary Clinton, as a fully paid-up member of the elite who was out of touch with the lived experiences of the white working class and more interested in appealing to the Obama coalition of communities of color, college graduates, and people who lived in large cities on the east and west coasts.

This chapter reflects on the challenge of choosing a president, drawing on our conversations with white working-class communities about their lived economic and social experiences, as well as their lived values. Rather than Trump's electoral success being the result of unconditional support from the white working class, our research shows a more nuanced set of findings. First, neither Trump nor Clinton were viewed as strong candidates, with many of our interviewees viewing the 2016 choice as problematic. Second, the Trump campaign became the conduit, or at least the platform, for the public voice of private disenchantment among sections of the white working class, including those across all sites in our research. Third, Trump successfully tuned into the working-class values that we have previously discussed in the book, for example, honesty, hard work, and directness, which helped him to frame and fix the political discussion, to which his opponent had to respond. Fourth, our data show that Clinton could not escape the negative labeling of dishonesty and being a member of the Washington elite. In short, her campaign tuned out of working-class values and was seen as a continuation of the politics as normal supported by elites.

Not all white working-class people voted for Trump

Our research was organized and implemented from September 2016 to April 2017. This was during the primary season, when both political parties were in the middle of a fractured selection process to decide who would be their nominees for the 2016 presidential election. The notion of class, and specifically the predicament of the white working class, was played out often and early during the primary campaigns. In the main, two individuals stood out as articulating a political program that: framed the political establishment as out-of-touch elites talking to themselves rather than the people; sharply critiqued large corporations as colluding with the government in neoliberal trade deals such as the North Atlantic Free Trade Agreement (NAFTA) that led to significant job losses and economic misery in working-class communities; and viewed globalization as leading to economic dividends for the wealthy and economic penalties for the poor. The ascent of these two individuals—Donald Trump and Bernie Sanders—based on promoting the concerns of white working-class people, contributed to both of them moving from the political wilderness to shaping the agenda of the Republican and Democratic parties specifically, and the US more generally.

Sanders took on the Democratic political establishment with an economically populist message that was a significant departure from the "Third Way" consensus of Bill Clinton and, to a lesser extent, Barack Obama. Rather than attempting to find a neoliberal consensus between capital and labor, Sanders railed against the excesses of large corporations and pinned the blame for the 2008 Great Recession on unaccountable capitalism. Although Sanders eventually lost out on the presidential nomination to the establishment-supported Hillary Clinton, his campaign nevertheless continued to have an impact on Democratic politics beyond the 2016 presidential campaign. The content and style of Democratic campaigns, seen most recently in the 2018 US midterms, have been marked by manifestos that speak about advocating on behalf of working-class communities, being critical of capitalism, and promoting economic populism.

Trump has arguably changed the politics of the US for many years to come. His performances in the Republican primaries were also underpinned by economic populism, though in conjunction with political nationalism. Similarly to Sanders, he cast himself as the insurgent candidate, separating himself from career politicians by highlighting his background in business and construction. The Trump message was direct and based on protecting the interests of workers against the damaging effects of NAFTA and trade deals with major partners such as China, as well as highlighting the security threat from uncontrolled immigration, especially from countries with Muslim populations and at the southern border with Mexico. This galvanized support among Republicans during the primaries and also among the electorate at large, leading to the shock result in November 2016 when he won the battle with Hillary Clinton to become President.

Following the general election, there was a splurge of commentary and analysis on the Trump triumph. The overarching narrative was that white working-class voters underpinned the success of Donald Trump having been won over by his successful mix of political populism and economic nationalism. This was encapsulated in the slogan "Make America Great Again," which was partly a recognition of the crisis facing the country, a lament and nostalgia for a past characterized by US hegemony, and a hope for a future of US renaissance. For example, *The New York Times* (2016) headlined an op-ed piece "Why Trump won: Working-class whites," with the following opening statement: "Donald J. Trump won the presidency by riding an enormous wave of

find it don't have already

support among white working-class voters." Similarly, J.D. Vance, the author of *Hillbilly Elegy* (Vance, 2016), wrote in *The Guardian* (2016) about an angry and disconnected white working class that connected with a messianic Trump:

> The white working class had grown angry: at the economy that failed to deliver good jobs, at the failed prosecution of two wars, at a government bureaucracy that failed to deliver good healthcare for veterans, at policy-makers who bailed out megabanks in the 2008 financial crisis even as many Americans lost their homes.

Vanity Fair (2017) also discussed the significant role of the white working class in flocking to Trump in unprecedented numbers. This view is evidenced as a victory for "forgotten white voters" (Donnan, 2016) and "a tonic for disaffected Americans" (Dorning, 2016).

However, a counter-argument emerged to challenge the prevailing view of the white working class. As Faber et al (2017) suggest, the notion that Trump won the White House because of a "Rust Belt Rebellion" is based on fake news—a term that has entered the lexicon. In addition, Silver (2016) makes the point that pinning the blame on the white working class for the success of Trump appears to be factually inaccurate given that the typical core supporter is much wealthier in terms of annual income than the average voter (earning $72,000 a year as opposed to £56,000 a year) and college educated. Sasson (2016) believes that the obsession of the media in pushing forward the view that white working-class communities powered the Trump campaign obscures the evidence of white and college-educated voters mobilizing to support the Republicans in 2016.

Following on from the counter-argument, our detailed research with 415 people across five different case-study sites demonstrates that the conventional wisdom of white working-class voters backing Donald Trump is too simplistic. Our work was based on organizing grass-roots focus groups with residents who were politically mixed and showed that the picture on the ground was much more complicated than the somewhat febrile national analysis.

Among the people that we interviewed, there was considerable skepticism of both presidential candidates. In fact, participants found significant failings in both Trump and Clinton. A phrase that was mentioned on numerous occasions during our discussions with white working-class communities was the problem in selecting the "lesser of two evils." Rather than the frequent media narrative of working-class communities supporting Trump in mass numbers, the focus group participants appeared to be genuinely conflicted about whom to support, as well as whether they should bother to vote at all when the reality of their lives under both Democrat and Republican presidents has been of reduced standards of living, the insecurity of the job market, and rising costs. White working-class people in our study certainly did not fit the description of a modern Praetorian guard for Trump, as some in the media had labeled them. Individuals were genuinely conflicted, and we found many instances of families, friends, neighborhoods, and communities taking up opposing positions, often blaming the partisanship of the 2016 campaign for the divisiveness. As the following participant commented in a focus group convened in Dayton, OH, characterized as the heart of the aforementioned "Rust Belt": "*I know very few people who are so straight one side or the other.... I think it's unfair to say everybody that supports him is of a specific [group]*" (Dayton FG).

The 2016 campaign was underscored by incendiary rhetoric on race and immigration, with much of it vented by Donald Trump. Sections of the population were identified as suspect groups, such as Muslims in the context of the "War on Terror" or Mexicans as "illegal migrants" or convicted criminals. Some of the national narrative viewed these racialized comments as being the type of language that enabled Trump to forge a bond with white working-class voters because it connected with their cultural fears. However, very few of the people we interviewed found this type of language to be acceptable when used by Trump, or, indeed, any other person. Rather our participants equated the rhetoric as boorish and juvenile: "*I can't stand a bully, but I am pro-Trump because Bernie's out of the race now*" (Dayton FG). Despite this participant categorizing Trump negatively as a bully, his vote was nevertheless cast for him. The quote also confers on Trump the mantle of being an outsider and as someone committed to taking on the vested interests of the establishment. As we discussed previously, there were similarities between Trump and Sanders in their analysis of the deterioration in living standards of working-class communities, the problems of globalization, and out-of-touch elites getting increasingly wealthy when the majority were suffering.

The interviewee just quoted was a Sanders-to-Trump switcher, moving from the populist Left to the populist Right. Although it would be incorrect to state that this type of change was a frequent occurrence across the case-study sites, neither was it the only time that it was mentioned by our participants. Both Trump and Sanders were the candidates for hope and change, albeit appealing to different communities outside white working-class groups. They placed themselves as authentic insurgents putting forward ideas to radically reform political debates and political systems. This was in contrast to the "politics as normal" that seemed to be presented by other candidates from the mainstreams of the Democrat and Republican parties.

Trump as a public voice for private disenchantment

The 2016 election presented white working-class communities as a naive and unthinking mass of people who turned to Trump through being seduced by his heady mix of cultural nostalgia and economic promises of returning jobs to industries that were in terminal decline. In more negative terms, the white working class is seen as the unstable precariat suggested by Standing (2011), being susceptible to swinging behind political extremism, or even a lumpenproletariat deemed as dangerous, useless, and devoid of class consciousness. They were the passive tools manipulated by a savvy businessman using his well-honed skills gained by presenting reality shows on network TV.

Yet, people in our study deeply resented being presented as puppets being pulled by a master puppeteer, as not understanding politics and policy, or, more bluntly, as being stupid and unthinking. Our own observations, whether from time spent with white working-class communities in the formal settings of focus groups, or from informally meeting and talking to people in Uber taxis, bars and diners, and a launderette, were to the contrary. We found voters sharply tuned to the political issues discussed by the candidates during the campaign. They viewed debates on television, analyzed commentary in the print media, and discussed politics with their family and friends on social media, as well as in everyday interactions, including with us as researchers. In contrast to an unthinking lumpenproletariat, the people we interviewed had strong views about politics and drew from their own experiences. This made the decision on which of the candidates to support very difficult for many because both Trump and Clinton had weaknesses. The following quote summarizes the point being made: "*I have actually read his entire platform, I am extremely familiar with what he's talking about, I just don't agree with it*" (Dayton FG).

In our study, the common and consistent view of both his detractors and supporters was that Trump was the public voice of private disenchantment. He captured an insurgent, anti-establishment rage against the "politics-as-normal" consensus that had held sway in the country for so long. Among participants across all sites, Trump managed to connect his message and align it to working-class values.

Participants perceived him as being "strong" and "hardworking" because he had successfully built the Trump organization, albeit with a significant amount of money from his family. Criticism of exploiting workers on construction sites and promoting anti-union activities failed to dent support among pro-Trump participants. They pointed out that he had dedicated his life to building successful businesses such as hotels and leisure complexes that created thousands of jobs for working-class communities in construction and laboring. Being demonized by the political establishment and not adhering to the norms of behavior expected of a presidential candidate did not lose him votes among the people we interviewed.

The manner in which Trump put across his political ideas during the 2016 election shocked the establishment as much as the content. By common consent, he was the most outlandish and outspoken candidate in modern political times, speaking on issues ranging from banning Muslims from migrating to the US, to erecting a wall on the southern border to keep out "illegal immigrants" and getting Mexico to pay for the construction, to accusing China of "raping" the US through taking advantage of preferential trade terms.

White working-class residents interviewed during our fieldwork were also appalled by this commentary. It did not represent them and they would not condone such language. Yet, at the same time, they recognized that he was a "straight talker," "direct," and "honest," which was in contrast with his opponents during the Republican primaries, and especially with Clinton during the presidential campaign. It should be noted that being "direct" and "honest" were important values that white working-class people expected from each other, as well as their elected representatives. The cruder language deployed by Trump during the 2016 campaign was excused by some on the basis that he was not a media-trained politician. Instead, he was "telling it as it was," and although they would not speak in this way themselves, they nevertheless saw this as grudgingly positive because Trump was unfiltered.

Those who supported Trump repeatedly mentioned his policies for protecting working-class jobs and communities, specifically his position on scrapping NAFTA, which had been viewed as leading to multiple factory closures across the country. Some of those we interviewed connected with key economic and working-class symbols of the campaign, for example, Trump donning a safety helmet and being flanked by miners at a June 2016 rally in West Virginia resonated with people. He promised to promote coal as a viable future energy source that would bring coalmining jobs back to the US. Another example of amplifying working-class insecurity was the Trump website playing a recording on a loop of a fractious meeting between bosses and employees at the Carrier air conditioning factory in Indianapolis that took place in February 2016. Here, a high-ranking executive from Carrier appears to be telling a large gathered group of angry employees on the shop floor of the decision to close the factory and relocate to Mexico. Unsurprisingly, the meeting erupted into angry insults toward bosses. These two examples played into the narrative of working-class communities as undeserving victims of NAFTA, with the prospect of a President Trump working hard to secure jobs.

In reality, it is going to be extremely challenging to maintain and grow mining as a sector in West Virginia or elsewhere in the US. The industry has been in long-term decline since 1980, with over 100,000 job losses, and although there has been a small increase in mining jobs since 2016, this is not statistically significant according to the US Department of Labor (see CNBC, 2018). With the help of tax credits, the Carrier factory in Indianapolis has remained open and not relocated to Mexico. However, nearly half of the 1,300 blue-collar jobs have been lost since 2016 and there is growing concern over future viability (*New York Times*, 2018). However, the symbolism of Trump being present in these working-class spaces, connecting with the concerns of working-class communities, and calling for policy interventions from government to prevent factory closures and save coalmines was not lost on many people we interviewed. In contrast to other political leaders, he appeared to be listening to concerns and advocating on behalf of working-class communities. In short, Trump had become the natural representative of white working-class concerns: the public voice of private disenchantment.

Throughout the interviews, the themes of anger, disenchantment, and need for economic and political change coursed through the discussions. The 2016 Trump campaign created a platform that enabled people to express concerns on a range of issues, including economic and political security, as well as the impact of immigration and change on lived experiences.

Importantly, they viewed the political and media elite as an oppressive force that had prevented white working-class communities from speaking openly about their concerns: "*We need a David to [slay] Goliath.... I thank God has given us our David and we should put him in and let him take the giant down*" (Bay Ridge FG). The previous quote was taken from a focus group in a neighborhood in Brooklyn, NY. The imagery is striking because it casts Trump not as a rich and celebrated businessman, but as a small David taking on the biblical giant Goliath against the odds, which is represented by fighting the political establishment, whether this is his Democrat opponent Hillary Clinton, the various establishment candidates that he took on and defeated in the Republican Party during the primaries, or the vested interests in the media who raged against him, such as the *New York Times* or CNN (Cable News Network).

Those who voiced support for Trump in our focus groups connected with the view of his candidature as being an outsider, someone that was sneered at by many and initially regarded as someone who was not worth taking seriously. In this way, it could be argued that they too felt ignored and reduced to being outsiders whose views were perceived to be out of alignment with an increasingly diverse and progressive country. For this participant and others, Trump opened up the possibility of challenging the political paradigm and hopefully changing it.

Trump as the public voice of private disenchantment was a strong and recurring message from those who supported him in our case-study sites. People viewed our research as an opportunity to vent about and support a candidate who was viewed as the most polarizing in modern history. The following quotes provide compelling insight into understanding his popularity: "*He's not a stupid man; he's showing you the disgust that the American people [feel]. They don't like it?! Too bad because this is how we all feel*" (Bay Ridge FG); "*He says what other people were thinking but they're too afraid to publicly speak*" (Dayton FG). The Trump campaign connected viscerally with the collective sentiment that at least someone had the courage and leadership to speak up and speak out about the impact of immigration on neighborhoods and an ailing economy on ordinary working people. Trump tapped into a deep well of grievances and concerns that had been building for many years. He had opened up a "Pandora's box" that was difficult for the establishment to close, however much they tried:

> 'He connected with what we're saying, we're talking about working class, he connected with working-class people … [we're] tired of … we send politicians there, the politician is 80 years old, he has got no connection to Joe out here in the middle of the country and here is this guy that comes in and he's talking to Joe.' (Tacoma FG)

In the previous quote from a focus group in Tacoma, a city steeped in working-class culture and heavily unionized, it is clear that Trump connected because of his agenda of focusing on American exceptionalism and talking about immigration and race relations, which others had avoided. The directness of his language may have offended many (including participants in our research) but many also admired him for raising issues that had been buried for too long. In contrast, mainstream politicians are painted as being out of touch with working-class people. They had neither the capability nor commitment to understand their lived experiences and articulate their concerns.

Some people in our interviews openly viewed the government and the media as suppressing or misrepresenting their views. In the following quote, again from Tacoma, this is expressed in a very direct way:

> 'They're scared about culture and security and then when I challenge them and said "Well, you don't think you're teetering on the very edge of being racist," they're horrified at the accusation. And what they say is … "Look at all this political correctness"…. We feel muzzled. We feel there's a chokehold on [the] throat of white people and white working-class people. We can't even say what we feel. That's the reason I voted for this guy, because he's actually saying this stuff that many people across America are thinking.' (Tacoma FG)

Here, a litany of problems is generated. People are muzzled by the omnipotent "political correctness," which is viewed as a device for preventing or closing down discussion and also placing white working-class communities as a racist and unthinking precariat. For some, Trump seemed to be allowing them to speak openly without being labeled as problematic or racist. He was outing concerns that had lain dormant for many years.

In the following quote from Birmingham, we see how white working-class people who took part in the research viewed Trump as being a straight talker and a different type of political leader intent on breaking up the establishment: "*Regardless of whether I agree with him or not, he's honest for the most part … isn't afraid to say anything, and that's the first time in my lifetime I have seen a politician say, 'You know what, I don't care. I'm going to say it*'" (Birmingham FG). The interviewee just quoted did not claim to be a Trump supporter, but it was notable that he was described as having values of being honest to some extent. Across all sites, when discussing working-class values, the virtue of being honest, and its corollary of communicating clearly and directly, resonated with people. As discussed previously, the many problems that people associated with Trump were counterbalanced by his ability to connect with communities who perceived themselves to have become disconnected, unheard, and ignored.

Trump understands the needs of the white working class

Trump is viewed almost as a messianic savior of the working class, as the following comment from a focus group in Birmingham, AL, demonstrates. There is an implicit assumption that the US obtained its status as a global power because of the hard work of working-class communities. Taking this further, it is suggested that the country has now fallen on more difficult times but could again be rescued by white working-class communities: "*If he can build that working class again, if he can get me a new factory back here, and we have more blue collar that will turn this country around.... I think that financially, if he can pull us up, the reason why I'm voting for him*" (Birmingham FG). As noted earlier, Trump's 2016 campaign was signposted by symbolic stops at working-class spaces, including coalmines and factories, where he spoke directly to coalminers and factory workers. His was not a technocratic campaign, but much more guttural and emotive, underlined by the message that "Make America Great Again" could be built on working-class jobs and working-class communities.

The disenchantment is not just related to the economy, but with political parties, which were viewed as having failed working-class communities. Some participants had grown up and had been socialized in staunchly Democrat families and households. They claimed to have only supported Democrat candidates locally and nationally. Yet, some were now of the view that the Democrats were the party of identity politics and were advocating on behalf of communities of color rather than white working-class communities. There was a sense that Democrats and Republicans alike had avoided engaging with white working-class communities because they were regarded as an outlier group in a modern, and increasingly ethnically diverse, country. The Trump campaign, and the candidate, directly connected with a range of economic and social concerns. To those who supported Trump in 2016, he was the "white" David who slew "the politically correct" Goliath:

> 'There is ... the feeling that working class has been alienated and marginalized ... so a lot of working-class people think that blacks in America are represented by the Democratic Party, and that their voice is being heard ... whereas [that] is not ... the case for the working class.... They're not talking

> about … the guy that's … working in Birmingham Steel.' (Birmingham FG)

The quote from someone who supported the Democrats in 2016 nevertheless demonstrates the perceived gulf between the party and the white working class. Birmingham Steel produced material that powered the Industrial Revolution in the US and helped to build the great modern cities such as Chicago and New York. Such was the importance of the industry that Birmingham became known as the "Pittsburgh of the South," employing 15,000 people at its peak, with the main employer being Sloss Furnaces. Now, only a single steel mill remains open in Birmingham. Steelworkers feel forgotten and left behind because no one appears to be engaging with them. This is consolidated by recent commentary from Birmingham about a proud legacy that is being lost. Trump recognized this while the Democrats either totally ignored it or were playing catch up: "Steelworkers often wonder if anyone still cares about this sector of Birmingham society.… They [steelworkers] know nobody cares, but we need to care because they are keeping alive what put Birmingham on the map" (*Alabama Opinion*, 2015).

white shift

Racialized views

Before and since the election of Donald Trump, there has been much discussion and debate on whether his election marked the racist last gasp of white working-class ascendancy in a country that is going to be minority white at some point in the 21st century (Glasser and Rush, 2016; Chotiner, 2017; McElwee and McDaniel, 2017). The participants who took part in our study were highly engaged and animated about the issues of class and race.

From the outset, it should be stated that racialized language was used in discussions by a minority of the participants. In a few instances, this was crude, and on some occasions, it was explicit; however, it was mostly racially coded by linking communities of color to references of crime, welfare dependency, and preferential treatment by the government in the competition for housing and jobs.

Some suggested that Trump gave legitimacy to people who held views that were anti-immigrant and against communities of color. Previously, these were much more difficult to express because they were viewed as unacceptable and, above all, racist: "*He gave a platform for a lot of people to come out and speak and they don't have to be nice*" (Phoenix FG).

Playing by the rules and not playing by the rules

A somewhat different perspective is provided by a participant from Dayton, who strongly disagreed with the correlation of Trump, and de facto the white working class, with racism. The media is blamed for "*a lot of generalization*." He stated unequivocally that his own experience within friends and family was that they are not racist, or in any way condone racialized language. In discussing immigration and strengthening the southern border with Mexico, the participant makes clear that he is not opposed to immigration, but simply wants immigrants to follow the law. This sentiment, differentiating between documented ("legal") and undocumented ("illegal"), was voiced on numerous occasions throughout the research and across the sites. Those who took this view stated that the US had historically been a country of immigration and that this had been to its advantage. A commonly held assertion was that people wanted documented migration to continue, and for individuals to be processed using legal channels so that those who may pose a security risk can be identified and rejected. The significant challenge was with undocumented migration. The rationale is that immigrants need to follow the rules, and that allowing undocumented immigrants unfettered access poses a security risk because the government does not know who is coming into the country:

> 'I think there's a lot of generalization going on here about those people that support Trump because it isn't plausible and I know a number of people who do support him and I would not consider them the least bit racist. Their issues are with security, and most of them like the idea but aren't the least bit bothered by immigration. They just want it done legally. You know, not in the night, across the river.' (Dayton FG)

Clinton's failure to connect with white working-class values

There were participants who took part in the research and identified as strong Democrats. They actively disliked Trump for being a Republican associated with the political extreme. However, for the most part, these same individuals showed little or no enthusiasm for their presidential nominee, Hillary Clinton. She did have some support among white working-class people but many of those interviewed did not support her personally, and sometimes had feelings bordering on visceral dislike.

Reflecting deeper on this view of Clinton, and also on the importance of working-class values, there was a sense that she was outside these beliefs, which were so important in shaping a sense of identity and belonging. Hillary Clinton was seen as a member of the political elite and as an "insider" offering "politics as normal" when the white working-class electorate seemed to be wanting hope and change. Across our study sites, we listened to consistent criticism leveled at Clinton and the Democrats that they had neither connected with the aspirations of white working-class people nor advocated on their behalf.

Some of those we interviewed (who were largely Trump supporters) felt that Clinton should not have been on the presidential ballot at all in 2016. The use of a private Internet server to send public emails appeared to some to be a blatant breach of the law that should have been prosecuted, and be punishable with a prison sentence. The alleged misuse of emails was more problematic because her non-conviction only served to underline that if you were wealthy and connected, a jail sentence could be avoided, whereas for working-class communities, the outcome would have been different:

> 'Anybody else, she would have been in jail, I am telling you right now, she's nothing but a disgrace to this country and if she wins, it's going to be disaster and it's going to be the same thing all over again. Politics aside, I can't stand it! I don't like her … she's very smug.' (Bay Ridge FG)

The issue that was mentioned was Hillary Clinton's perceived involvement in the deaths of US citizens, including the US Ambassador in Benghazi, Libya, in 2012. The episode was raised a number of times as "Benghazi" and consolidated the view that Clinton, along with the email episode, could not be trusted and was fundamentally dishonest: "*She doesn't deserve to be in this country; I think she is a treasonist. I think she is a baby killer and I think she shouldn't be here. I don't think she should be on the ballot paper*" (Dayton FG). Clinton was seen as being opposed to working-class values: "*Hillary is … a liar, a cheat, you can't trust her. At least we know … what Trump's going to do. Also, honesty, like the working-class value*" (Birmingham FG).

White working-class people in our study felt disconnected from her because she represented the political elite, "insiders," and Washington. Her language and campaign appeared to forget about white working-class voters, instead preferring to appeal to college graduates, minorities, and the urban middle class. The sense was that her life experiences and varied roles in politics, including First Lady, US Senator, and US Secretary of State, confirmed her as part of the establishment and not related to the lived experiences of working-class communities:

> 'Then she gets up there and talks, she opens her mouth … ignorant and stupid. I mean some of the things she says is just … she is so disconnected; she just doesn't know.… Is that because they've been, the leadership … in politics … in Washington DC too long and haven't been back out to the communities to where the working class is at and connected to them? They haven't.' (Tacoma FG)

> 'She's a career politician who has [bloated] her coffers on the generosity of others, the working-class people.' (Birmingham FG)

During the 2016 election campaign, Clinton stated that some of Trump's supporters were "Deplorables" because of their xenophobic, sexist, and homophobic views (Jacobs, 2016). The sense that white working-class voters were racist jarred many of those who participated in our research. Participants eagerly pointed out the ethnic diversity of their family and network of friends, as well as how they supported work colleagues who were being subjected to racial and sexual harassment. Indeed, many had voted for the first black president in 2008.

"Deplorable" became a form of cultural resistance against a sneering and out-of-touch elite. Indeed, people who attended Trump rallies during the 2016 campaign wore T-shirts emblazoned with "I am a Deplorable." Clinton made matters worse with her pronouncements about moving to cleaner fuels instead of boosting coalmining. These were the very same workers who were being championed by Trump. This seemed to underline that she could not understand or empathize with some white working-class people:

> 'She made a mistake when she was down in Pennsylvania, or in, no, West Virginia, where she says, "Oh, we've got to do away with the coalminers." That went over like a brick.' (Bay Ridge FG)

> 'This election is on a lot of people's minds because, you know, my one friend, the other day, she was almost in

> tears, Hillary got nominated, I'm going to have to sell all my property because she's going to raise all my taxes.' (Dayton FG)

> 'Well, as I said, and I'm a registered Republican, I've been one my whole life. And if he was running against someone other than Hillary, some other woman.... I am all for a woman president. I have no problem with that at all, but Hillary is a different situation. The Clintons are a different situation due to their track record. I distrust her more.' (Bay Ridge FG)

These final two quotes from Dayton in Ohio and Bay Ridge in New York City demonstrate how some participants conjoin the prospect of higher taxes under Clinton together with an acute distrust of "the Clintons." The combination of visceral dislike, distrust, and disconnection prevented Clinton from being embraced or liked even by people who voted for her.

Conclusion

The 2016 election intersected with our fieldwork and provided a backdrop to the discussions with white working-class communities across our case-study sites, both before and after the US election. In many respects, it could be put forward that the election was about hope and change, and was in this way similar to the historic election of 2008, which led to the first person of color, Barack Obama, being elected President. While acknowledging some similarities between Obama and Trump in that they were both outsiders and led insurgent campaigns against Hillary Clinton—indeed, there were some Obama to Trump switchers in our fieldwork—it is also the case that there were considerable differences in the content of policy and how it was delivered as a political message. In 2016, Trump was about hope and change for white working-class people and understanding that they felt ridiculed, silenced, and left behind in the context of making progress and nation building. As we discussed, the symbolism of Trump maximizing working-class anxiety in spaces such as a coalmine and donning a miner's helmet, or promising to keep the Carrier air conditioning factory open in Indianapolis rather than letting it relocate to Mexico, was recognized and appealed to many participants in our research.

The conventional view of white working-class voters mobilizing en masse for Trump was not always borne out in our fieldwork. Many had considerable concerns about his character and capability that prevented them from voting for him. It should also be noted that white working-class people continued to support the Democrats. However, we found deep concern about Hillary Clinton, bordering on active dislike from her opponents as well as those in the study who identified as Democrats. From our perspective, the 2016 election was a messaging campaign between who could align themselves with perceived white working-class values and what it means to be working class, including being honest, using direct language, and working hard. It was clear that candidate Trump keyed into these values and highlighted white working-class concerns as part of a broader messaging on the economy and expressions of cultural insecurity. He did this by references to the failures of NAFTA and globalization, as well as the threat from Muslims and Mexicans. Clinton was a perfect opponent for Trump in 2016. She was perceived as an elite member disconnected from the experiences of white working-class communities, as seen by her labeling of them as "deplorable." Her message of "politics as normal" had not changed from when her opponent was Obama in 2008, when the country called out for change. In 2016, she had the political baggage of being part of the "Clintons," which repelled many in our research through the inference of people on the make and take.

Going forward to post-2020, politics needs to be organized differently. It is clear that white working-class communities view themselves as being left behind, not just economically, but also politically. Political organizations need to reach out to these voters and reconnect with their fears and concerns. This means moving beyond the elite-versus-elite discussions—moving from "grasstops" to "grassroots"—in order to listen to the lived experiences of working-class communities. At a moment in time when our participants, and, indeed, people around the world, have limited or no trust in their political representatives, and traditional party-political organizations are crumbling in some countries, the success of the post-2020 and post-Trump politics could be based on those who seek to see voters as neither Republicans nor Democrats, but simply as voters. Working across the blurring of political allegiances demands a paradigm shift in thinking as it dismantles decades of political tactics. However, as the 2018 midterms showed across different campaigns, from Texas, to Florida, to New York, those candidates who present in a different way often have the most success at the polls.

In the future, the challenge of choosing a president will rest on building a different type of hallowed "rainbow coalition" in which white working-class communities could, and should, be a critical and an important section—no longer "deplorable," but a successful building block that helps the country to deal with a problematic past and a changing, uncertain future. The experiences of being white and working class now and in the immediate response to a new national leader is the theme of Chapter 5, represented by a focus group undertaken soon after the inauguration of Donald Trump as President. The chapter illuminates many of the themes that emerged from the myriad conversations that we held with white working-class people.

5

Talking about race, identity, and change

Introduction

This chapter offers an insight into a group discussion with residents on the broad themes of the research study. In Chapter 4, we showed how both Trump and Clinton were viewed during the election campaign, and how Trump was sometimes viewed as understanding and representing the white working class. Trump was seen as able to understand and articulate what had been lost and how it could be regained through slogans and vitriolic talk. Trump understood what Hochschild (2016) called the "deep story": the story of "strangers in their own land" able to emerge as "strangers no longer." Similar to our research, Hochschild's investigation found people divided over Trump: some supported him and some did not. In our research, the "deep story" was of Trump being able to represent and articulate a public voice of private disenchantment among some sections of US voters.

The following discussion was held in a home in a city about 20 miles away from Phoenix, Arizona, situated within Maricopa County. While Phoenix is largely a Democrat city, Maricopa County is staunchly Republican. President Elect Trump lost nine of the ten largest counties in the US on election day but was victorious in Maricopa. Indeed, Maricopa County was reported as the most pro-Trump county in the US.

Organized by a local resident and involving six people (five female; one male), the discussion occurred soon after the inauguration of President Elect Trump on January 20, 2017. Taking a taxi from downtown Phoenix and leaving the sprawling city that stretches for miles, it took some 40 minutes to reach the location where this conversation would be held. Arriving in the dark, the sense was that the area was deeply residential, separate from the city of Phoenix and expanding. Arriving as a lone researcher and not from the US, there was a level of anxiety about how I would be received even though the event had been organized by a key informant who would also be attending the discussion. I had heard from some people of color in the US that they felt uncomfortable immediately after the election. How would I be received?

Ringing the front doorbell, I was welcomed into the family home; pizzas had been delivered and the participants had arrived. Wellman (1977: 74) had claimed that "most sociologists would not recommend that black people interview whites," and as discussed in Chapter 2, this had been a concern of ours. Hochschild (2016: 250) had similarly stated that "it helped, I think, that I was white, female, gray-haired" in her more recent research on the American Right, that is, that she would be seen as less threatening, softer, and approachable in focusing on a topic of concern that was also central to her participants. Our research, and certainly the following discussion, highlights that being non-white was not a barrier: a bearded British-Indian man could gain access and the trust of strangers in a different land.

The group discussion started with the general preamble regarding research ethics, understanding and completing consent forms, gaining permission to record the discussion, their right to withdraw, and the purpose of the research. The discussion lasted about 75 minutes and while presented in the following in an edited format, it offers the reader an insight into a moment captured at the intersection of a shift in power, discourse, and presidents.

Experiences of living in the neighborhood

I: *Thank you for agreeing to be part of this focus group. It would be useful if you said your name and how long you have lived in the area, what you like about it?*

F1: I have lived in the neighborhood for a year, exactly, I think. What I like about it? My kids can go out and play. It's huge because they couldn't where we used to live. Just, it's not really hard to … you don't really come across people that are just irate, upset, high strung, like in California how it was. …

Yes. I moved from California, and so then we moved out here and I started waitressing so I really was around people and just the people in general, I just really enjoy them. Just the class, it's awesome, it's so much better.

F2: Hi. We've lived in this neighborhood 13 years, just on 13 years, and I love this neighborhood. It's home, I guess, is the main thing and we know everybody and, I guess, like F1 said, I love that my kids can just go play and, for the most part, feel safe, and I like that we're away from the city. That's probably the main thing. I don't like living near the city.

I: *What do you define as the "city" here?*

F2: Downtown Phoenix. The busy traffic. I don't like being around that. I've been away from that.

F3: I have lived in Arizona but not here, Gilbert, over there, since 2007. I had a year hiatus in the middle, but, ultimately, 2007, and I've been in the same neighborhood the whole time, most of it. I love where I live because it's very family oriented and there are a lot of kids. It's very safe. My kids play out all the time. I don't have to worry, like, they're out. I can kick them out and they'll play and I'm not really … even my five year old, I'm not super-worried about her being out front and playing. They can walk to school. There are parks, there are bypaths, there's a lot of … just, away from the city, as well. I like the city but I don't think I would feel comfortable living there with my children. So that's about it.

F4: I also live on the other side of downtown Phoenix and Mesa, and I really like my neighborhood because I know all my neighbors. We can get together, we have dinners, we have different pot lucks, and if I need anything, I know that I can go to any of my neighbors in my neighborhood and talk to them about anything. Like, I needed my car jumped when my grandma left and I went over to one of my neighbors and I was like, "Can you jump my car for me?" He was like, "Yeah, sure." It's just stuff like that. We can just go to each other whenever we need anything, and that's why I like my neighborhood.

F5: I live down the road here in the next development. I've lived there for over ten years now and I like my neighborhood because I do feel safe. There is a sense of peace and quiet when I go home every night and I do know my neighbors but I'm the only one in my family that's actually got to know my neighbors, so that kind of makes it difficult in my household, but I enjoy the sense of comfortability and safeness that I feel when I live there.

M1: I enjoy living here. I chose this neighborhood, new construction, back about 13 years ago and I chose it because it was on the outskirts of downtown Phoenix. It's a suburb, a new construction, so all the structures, all the businesses, all the facilities and resources are all new, modern, I really enjoy that, and the conveniences are all here, local. I don't have to travel into Phoenix, very rarely. Everything is available here within a 15-minute drive, you know? Restaurants and shopping centers and all that kind of stuff, and it's very family oriented. The elementary schools and the high schools are in a real close proximity. Children don't have to ride the bus. They can walk to school, and it's relatively safe. The crime is low and I feel very comfortable here.

The meaning of "white working class"

I: *How would you define "white working class"? What does it mean to you?*

F3: It's a good question.

M1: My first impression of "white working class," obviously, the definition of race, "white." The second, "working class," to me, says individuals that need to have gainful employment continuously in order to provide their living for their children. They don't have a family that has an affluent family that provides economic security where they wouldn't have to work, or substantial inheritance, or things like that. That's what "white working class" means to me.

F2: Yes, when I think of working class, the white obviously, to me, would mean race but when I think of the working class, I think of those who are at that point in their life where they're still supporting either themselves or a family and have not reached that retirement point. Or, are not disabled or in a position that they don't have to work, whether that be inheritance, or are not self-sufficient.

F3: I wonder if we could add, possibly, I don't know, like, not a business owner, not a corporate executive, not an upper echelon of power in a work structure, but more maybe middle management, middle administration, or under. But when I think of working class, I think of someone who is not yet at that, but that's debatable, I don't know.

F5: That is debatable. Yes, or sustainable employment, working toward bettering themselves or their family, I think, is very important. There is always that consistency, that strive to do better, that strive to give your family more. I think that plays within the working class. That's what I was thinking of when she was talking.

I: *Striving? How do you evidence that in yourself?*

F5: Myself? Well, I grew up with parents that started from the bottom of the company that they went into and they worked their way up. My mum is a perfect example of that. She started as a bagger in a grocery store and now she works in corporate and makes over six figures a year. That always, "I can do better, I can do more, I can put in more hours, I can always achieve the best, what I'm doing…." Unfortunately, she's always said, "What I'm doing is not good enough." That also is playing a big part in it too.

I: *What do you think about that?*

F1: Honestly, I'm having a hard time with this [laughter] and that's only because of a recent change in my life that is … okay, I almost didn't come because I'm just very overwhelmed with me not working right now. So, I would say, working class, yes, I'm at home working, constantly working. Getting nothing done. It's a thankless job, you know? I'm staying at home and then you can always do better but I didn't get an education and I'm not planning, in the near future, to get one, so I feel, kind of, defeated a little bit at this moment. But I know that the most important job is in the home, but I need to make some money. It's just tough, so I'm thinking, "Oh, my gosh, white working?" I'm not even … I'm poverty list. It's just where I'm at right now.

F2: It's true.

F1: You know what's crazy? I've been in the yard just pulling weeds. There is so much work, my back is killing me, so if I'm going like this … it's because I'm in pain, and I just want to … I am, I am in pain. I think what's contributing to this pain, not only do I have a lot of back pain, but I think it's the stress, the muscles, and it's just all right there.

F2: Isn't that part of being working class? Because you would have had to pull the weeds whether you were working, or not.

F1: Yes, and I don't mind doing it. I don't mind working. My dad always said, "It doesn't matter what job you have as long as you do the best you can do at it."

I: *The notion of living paycheck to paycheck. Many people have said that in other interviews, and I just wondered if that resonates with you in terms of the working class?*

F2: Yes, I don't think it matters how much you make; you spend what you make. You get a raise and you're like, "Where did that go? I was looking forward to that extra. Where did it go?"

F3: I was going to talk to that point that I feel, and I don't know because just my awareness is growing, the middle class is getting, I don't know, well, I think I am getting lower and lower in this ability to get out of this position. So, I don't know. Obviously, I just come and accept this is where I am and this is what it's going to be like, or this is just a period of time of my growth in where I am or because of my situation with my family and that, and all the hats that I wear. So, I feel there's a burden from the outside as well, as far as the cost of what one needs, food costs, getting places, childcare costs, healthcare costs, there are so many obstacles that get bigger.

I: *Is that a bigger burden, do you think, for people who would define themselves as white working class or working class?*

F3: I think there's a stratification where those who meet certain income guidelines, have some assistance available and sometimes it's not good enough but those that don't have a need because they can do it … and then there's nothing for those in between and I find that gets bigger and bigger because the resources get pushed down further because there is so little, and then these have much more wealth and they can do much more than those in the middle. It's encompassing and it's hard to, I think, get people to understand that and to think of real solutions for that.

I: *But you said something really interesting as well, about "stuck," and it's similar in a sense to what F1 said?*

F1: Totally.

I: *Do you think working class is "stuck," that "I feel that it doesn't matter how hard I work, I might not be able to change this reality," or is it just a point in time?*

F1: I think of it every day. That's my reality. I know anything could happen but, realistically, I'm alright with it. As long as we have our ends meet, I don't care. I had a mum, a step-mum, that stayed home and that was the best thing ever. But, yes, being stuck because, "Oh, you don't work?" Yet you're supposed to … that income, and then if you're on assistance, not only do you feel, like, terrible about it. You don't want it to be that way, but, yes, stuck. But then, like, insurance is $800 a month. I mean, Jeeze! Really? I can't afford it, so I don't like the fact that my kids have to go on access. You know what I mean? I don't. I have family that are very wealthy but they earned it, just like I have to. I don't see the light at the end of the tunnel, but that's okay, but it shouldn't be like that. I should have made better choices because it's only my fault that I feel like I'm stuck, do you know what I mean? We weren't supposed to have kids, and I have four, so things change [laughter].

Making choices between work and family

M1: I think the "stuck" is a relative term and I think all of us could get unstuck but I believe that we would have to make some significant sacrifices, ie, family, that we wouldn't be willing to make.

I: *What do you mean?*

M1: Essentially, because you can't really … well, you can just walk away but that's ideally what you would have to do in some cases, or be pretty much absent and working all the time, in order to get to a level where you are above that and sacrificing more time at work, less time at home, less time with the family.

F3: But those relationships are everything.

F5: Exactly.

M1: I could spend 80 hours at work if I wanted to and the company would pay me and they would be "Great job, you're here, you're so dedicated," but at home, I'd be non-existent.

F3: Without relationships, there's nothing. If I have a good relationship, then I can say that I would be more than content if my relationships with the people, my children, my family, and I have people that I feel I connect to and I have an identity as to who I am, then I think it's a great place to be. But if I had to pick, if I could be more financially better at the expense of people, I don't think I'd choose that.

Limits of the American Dream

F4: Well, my brain is just, like, turning really quickly but it's interesting to hear this conversation because I'll be entering the workforce really soon in a professional manner.

F2: But you do work.

F4: Well, I do work, yes, but I mean for myself and on my own and be self-sufficient, I will soon. But anyway, I think this is the whole idea of our society right now about having the best of everything, the most of everything, the newest of everything, and how some people sometimes prioritize that over their family, over their relationships, over what is actually important and how what you do sometimes isn't good enough, and also that turnover of how it changes so quickly. People are trying so hard to keep up with that. They are caught up in it. I think that plays a big role in it too. I hate to say it, but I think materialism plays a huge part in our society and why we try and get what we want and what we feel is important because if we have the newest iPhone, the best car, for a moment, it makes us feel like we've earned it, or that we're better than someone else, or that we deserved it for ourselves. We achieved it.

F3: What she just said is all part of this American Dream ideology and right now, I'm in the workforce, I work full time and I'm also a full-time student. So, going back to what you were saying before about living paycheck to paycheck, I put half of my paycheck every week that I earn, I put it into my savings account so, that way, I can get out of school debt free and so, right now, if I were to stop doing that, yes, I would be a lot more better off but I would also be thousands and thousands of dollars in debt. I paid over $11,000 to go to school this year....

So, I am doing this whole living from paycheck to paycheck and, again, my grandma has been my rock this entire time. She's allowing me to stay at home rent free and she helps me do as much as she possibly can. She's actually getting extremely sick right now, which is unfortunate, but that's another story. Anyway, she's allowing me to do this so I'm building stronger relationships with employers and my grandmother and my aunt, and I'm actually getting a really good relationship with my mother that I never had before in the past, and that still sucks. I don't have ... I feel like I'm working so much not to have anything and I feel like that's also a big part but I also have the ideology of this American Dream that I started off, which is that I really want something and I feel like I'm working hard enough to get it, but I just don't have it.

I: *That's really amazing, well done.*

F3: Thank you. So far, I'm in my third year of college and I'm just going to ... I already have my next semester paid for, almost. So, I only have about $1,000 left that I have to pay for and my next semester is done.

Defining "working class"

I: *One way that working class is defined is, for example, somebody, in this case we're talking about white as a race, white without a college degree, would be working class. What do you think about that?*

F1: Not true. Most of the people here are either studying or have got a degree.

F5: Everybody here says not true but that mum that I just mentioned didn't even graduate high school, the one that makes over six figures who worked as a bagger

	and went all the way to corporate. She didn't even graduate high school.
F1:	My dad, the same thing.
F5:	Oh yes, I mean, she's definitely an exception. There's no doubt about it. I guess we could talk about exceptions all day.
F3:	Well, my parents too didn't go to college.
F1:	Yes, the only one out of six kids, the only one that graduated was me and the only one that doesn't ... everybody else makes money and they make a lot of it, so it's like....
I:	*Okay, what about then working class is defined as "people who earn less than $52,000 a year?"*
F2:	Oh, no.
M1:	No, I wouldn't agree with that either.
F3:	No. I would say the threshold is higher.
F5:	Yes, I would think it's higher.
F2:	Substantially.
I:	*So, you and many other people think about the notion of working class very differently to how it's measured in terms of policy or by government.*
F3:	100 per cent, I can tell you. So, this is what we say. People who make policy or people who practice from the admin side but never worked on the low side don't understand what it is to do the work. So, I think those that make definitions about certain things that don't have the practical side are not really getting a full look at things and don't see it from diverse perspectives.

Neighborhood diversity

I:	*Is this a mixed community? Do different classes live here, different racial groups? What's it like?*
F2:	Yes. There are different sections to Surprise. There is what we call the Copper Canyon [laughter].
F5:	Yes, I know what you're talking about.
F2:	Which is, like, the wealthy area. The homes are the multi-million-dollar-homes area. Then there's the old Surprise area.
M1:	It used to be the farming community.
F5:	Yes it did.

F2: Yes, thank you, I wasn't quite sure how to soften that. Then, there's like this area which I guess you would say is your middle-class area which is everybody....

F1: Diverse as far as race.

F2: There's that too.

F1: I don't notice that.

F5: I was just about to say the same thing. I don't notice that either.

F1: I'm saying I don't notice that because the last school in California, my kids were the only white kids that were walking around and I'm not racist, it doesn't bother me, but it just so happened to me that I could easily pick out my kid because he's the one ... you know what I mean? Very rare, very few.

I: *You mean, back in California?*

F1: California. Coming here, I don't notice. I just notice they're all just white kids, or Mexican, I guess.

M1: It's very diverse.

F1: Yes, I guess it is. I just notice there is a big difference in the way that people are here, as far as race is.

F3: Not as diverse as it was.

F1: That's not even as bad, like, you don't hear, you know, there's not a bunch of friction about them. Everybody is just cool with everybody. I notice that.

F3: Interesting perspective. Interesting, see, I live down the street, and I might remind you that where I went to high school is different to where their kids are going to high school, and we lived just one street, like, one major street away from each other, and we only have one African-American family that lives on our street. We're all white on our street and we're all white on the street next door. So, it's interesting to hear these guys say that they have diversity, and then I'm across the main street, and I'm saying that we don't. So, I mean, I don't think we have enough. We had some Latino and African-American or black students in our school but it was definitely, predominantly white. I wished it was more diverse at the high school that I was at.

I: *Okay, thank you. What about Phoenix, generally, then? Is it segmented with different ... like, I've been doing some work up in Maryvale. I don't know if you know Maryvale, which has changed very dramatically since the 1950s?*

F2: It has, yes.

F5: Maryvale, metro, South Phoenix.

M1: Yes.

I: *So, there are places, you're naming places. What's in those places that you're naming?*

F5: Well, metro Phoenix has quite a bit of diversity, and so does South Phoenix, more than the usual here in the valley because of the amount of resources that are there, and the people that live there. We have a lot of refugees. We have a lot of recent immigrants that live down there. We have a lot of unaccompanied minors that live in that area. Those two, predominantly, that's where most of our resources in the valley are at. So, that's why I named those two in particular. Maryvale has, particularly, a lower socio-economic status than the rest of the valley so they have some … they actually have quite a mix down there. I mean, I have family who live down there and they have Latino neighbors down the street, and black and white.

F3: We lived down there for a while.

F5: They have some mixture in there, in Maryvale, so that's why I was naming those three places in particular.

Diversity as an everyday experience

F4: I live in Mesa. Mesa and Gilbert, I would say there are a lot of Mormons that live out there but what I notice, like, when I went to high school, we had a very, very large Latino Hispanic population. That was the majority of our school, and then we had so it was pretty much the Hispanic, and then it went to the African-American and black community and then, I would say, the Caucasian would be the lowest numbers at my high school. …But, for me, since I grew up with that, because I've lived in Mesa for 21 years, I'll be 21 in a week, so I've lived there.…

But, yes, for me, I just don't really know how to describe it. I guess, I just grew up with it, with the different, the diversity too. So, for me, I don't really notice it as much but, at the same time, I notice it at the same time because all my friends are all different ethnicities and races and all that, but I don't really have any friends that are of the same race as me. All mine are different ethnicities and ages, and it's just, kind of, when I look at it, I'm like, "Wow!" I think I have one friend, two friends, out of my whole entire, everyone that I talk to, that I am close to, that are white. Everybody else has some kind of different ethnicity, race, and some kind of different background to myself. So, it's kind of different over there, in Mesa.

F3: I was just going to … I don't know what I was going to say [laughter]. We do have diversity but I think coming from an outside perspective of living in the East Coast, it gives me a different viewpoint of how I see our city and just for being such a big city, not just 500 square miles, but the population compared to inner America, I think it's not as diverse as one would think it could be for the size and capacity that we have, but there is a diversity. But, at the same time, it's not, when you look at it from other perspectives and other cities, it isn't as much.

Rural to urban growth and development

F3: It has changed in a couple of years. Even if you just stop at five years. I mean, I can't go much further back, but just in the five years, I've noticed a lot of changes.

M1: Huge growth.

F3: Which is interesting to see the fast growth in a small short time. I can't speak big time changes, but….

M1: Well, 13 years ago in this particular spot, you would have been sitting in a field [laughter].

F2: Well, just right in this area, huge, yes.

M1: This entire city was nothing but farmland 20 years ago. I've lived here 28 years and I used to drive from Litchfield Park North to Bell Road and this was nothing but open grass and fields and agriculture, and I still remember pretty much anything west of 75th Avenue was pretty much empty also. There was a lot of farmland, so huge amounts of road in the city.

F3: Building so fast.

M1: It just enormously has been developed, but we're relatively a very young state, you know?

F2: Yes, 100 years, right?

M1: So, 1912 was pretty much … it's just been 100 years.

I: *We're talking about Arizona here?*

M1: Yes, Arizona itself, and the Phoenix metropolitan area and we talk about Maryvale back in the 50s. That was a farming community but now it's considered part of metropolitan Phoenix. So, just huge amounts of growth in a very small period of time.

Self, memories, and change

I: *What does that do to you, for your own sense of self, for example?*

F1: Well, I had total goosebumps when he was talking. Wow! That's right and I've just realized that.

F2: It's true though, yes. Even Maryvale, we were talking about Maryvale. I lived in Maryvale in the 90s and it was questionable in the 90s, but I was driving through it, the old Maryvale mall area, the other day, and it is so different than it used to be back then. I mean, the whole mall thing has gone. I actually called you and I was like, "The Maryvale mall has gone!"

M1: It's been gone for years. I used to work there, long ago.

F5: Once upon a time.

F2: He's like, "Of course it's gone." I'm like, "It's a Walmart."

I: *When you saw that, what did that mean to you, how did that make you feel, then?*

F2: Strange, yes. I guess, strange….

It's changed. It's changed. I don't know, weird, I guess, because I don't want to say "My old stomping ground" because that just sounds odd, but what's normal and just what you are remembering has just gone and now they've put up Walmart. I mean, really? Walmart? I don't know.

M1: To me, the growth is kind of exciting. I moved here from North-Western Montana so when I came to visit the Phoenix area for the first time, I just saw it as opportunity. So, to me, when I see growth, when I see things building, it's more opportunity, more things to do. I'm waiting for the fields just a little bit west of here where they have planned developments of shopping centers and things. I'm waiting, "When are they going to build a Circle K on my corner so I've got, you know, a place to get gas," or more developments. I'm looking for things to be finished and completed, so, to me, the growth is exciting, new things happening, new people coming into the area. I see it as opportunities and exciting.

F4: My neighborhood was at its peak in the 90s and I grew up right next to Fiesta Mall and I know when I was in junior high … so that was back in 2008/09 [laughter].

F3: She had to think way back for that! [Laughter.]

F4: Yes, I'm trying to think, but I remember when I was in junior high, we used to all go down, after school, we'd all go down to the mall to hang out. That was our place to meet new people, and to build friendships and everything, and now it's closed. There are two stores, I think, that are still there and that mall used to be the best place to be, especially in the 90s. My high school used to be the biggest high school in Arizona and now it's probably one of the tiniest. The high school population in my neighborhood is decreasing dramatically every year. My mum, she went to my high school and when she graduated, she had a couple of thousand kids in her graduating class and in my graduating class, we had about 550. So, just in 20 years, my neighborhood has just plummeted. Not plummeted, but it's getting older. The residents are getting older. There are no more young kids coming.

F3: They're moving out further.

F4: They're trying to revitalize that area though, so that way we can bring more young people back in, so not everything crashes.

Experiencing belonging

I: *What does "belonging" mean to you? How do you know you belong? You can have any geographical space. It could*

	be belonging in your neighborhood, or belonging in the bigger Phoenix.
F4:	I feel like I belong because I was born here. I've never lived out of state. I've lived in my house since I was born so I feel my sense of belonging starts because I've lived there for so long. I've known all my neighbors since I could talk, since I was a baby. They've all met me since I was born, so I feel like my sense of belonging is just because I've been there for so long. I've built those relationships since I was a baby up until now. So, I think that's where my sense of belonging comes from. My neighborhood and where I'm from.
I:	*But your community has changed as well, you were saying.*
F4:	It has changed.
I:	*Do you still feel the same strength of belonging?*
F4:	I do. I feel like because everybody is growing older, I think the relationships are getting stronger, you know what I mean? Because, now, some of the people that live on my street, they are all retired, so now those bonds are starting to become tighter because now they're going out for lunch and they're going and doing this together, and doing that together, instead of going to work, coming home, doing the housework, and going to bed. So, that's how I view it. That's where our sense of belonging I can feel in my neighborhood is coming from.
F2:	I probably would say, for me, my sense of belonging in my area, in this state, is just more within me than exterior. It's how I feel. It's a comfort. If there is something going on that makes me feel uncomfortable with my environment, then I don't feel like I belong. It could be just walking outside my home. If there is a big party going on outside and I feel uncomfortable with it, I don't feel like I belong. If there is a lot of traffic or something like that and I am uncomfortable with it and I don't want to drive in it, then I don't feel like I belong. So, it's not necessarily external as much as it's internal.
I:	*Something "I feel?"*
F2:	Yes.

F1: You explained that very, very good. I can totally relate to that.

F2: I'm that type of person.

M1: Can you repeat the question?

F5: What do you feel when you belong? What does it mean to you?

M1: Familiarity in a surrounding area. You always feel, when you leave your home area, however many circumference of miles that may be, when you start to get out of your comfort zone, when things don't look familiar any more, that kind of helps me feel where I belong. If I go into downtown Phoenix to run an errand or something, I don't feel like I belong. I feel like I'm a visitor to that area, but then as soon as I start to get back in the Surprise area in my town, I see things that are familiar, street signs, shopping centers.

F2: You see, I can drive downtown, even in Mesa, and feel completely okay.

M1: I feel okay.

F2: If I am comfortable.

M1: But I don't feel like I belong there. To me, that's someone else's city, someone else's town, someone's community. This, I feel this is my town, this is my community. I feel like I belong. I feel like I have some ownership and I think it's all built on my familiarity with the surrounding area.

I: *Is it also because you're coming home to your...?*

F2: Yes, that could be.

M1: Yes, and it gets stronger as you get in closer. You can talk about the Surprise area, I feel like I belong, but then when I get into my subdivision, I really feel like, "I'm comfortable here." Then, of course, when you get home, that's another feeling in itself.

F5: That's a good point that you brought up about familiarity, but also, I feel like your sense of belonging also feels like where you feel that you fit in, in the environment perspective. Because, me, I'm the opposite. I'm somebody that's living in a suburb and I'm in my young 20s and all I want to do is go out and all I want to do is be around people and all I want to do is see new things and I want to meet new people all the time. I go out a lot, but it's not around here because it's just not here. Which is fine, if that's what you want. That's what my parents want and that's why they live here, but I'm telling you, once I get my degree, I'm moving out of here because it's just not for me.

F2: She's like, "I'm out!"

F5: It's a great neighborhood and it's great to raise a family or retire but if you're in your young 20s and you're like me and you like that adventure and that diversity and that conversation and meeting new people all the time, this isn't the place. So, that's why I feel more … what was the term that you used?

F2: Belonging.

F5: Belonging in the east side because the east valley really has that more, I feel, than the west side.

F3: I look at it in two ways. Just me, as a person, when I feel I have a purpose and I have a value or a connection to something and what I do has a meaning and relevance somewhere in life. But as far as my community as well … I'm renting, so sometimes, I'm debating, "Should I buy, should I move?" But this community, I feel so tied to just being in the same … because I've been established for so many years there. I know the neighbors, the school, the area, so I feel comfortable. That level of comfort just in that geographic area.

Trump connecting with the white working class

I: *Thank you. There was this strong sense that Donald Trump had really connected with this group of people we call "white working class" and I was just wondering what your sense of that was? Did he, didn't he, what was going on do you think?*

M1: I don't think he necessarily connected.

F2: No.

M2: I believe….

F2: That's not the right word.

M1: With the white working class, people were seeking change, looking for something different, and the white working class felt they were stuck in this continuum and they felt like, maybe, he would possibly be a change to push something in a different direction, and I think that's what they were looking for. It wasn't necessarily anything connected to him, or the things he said, or … maybe he drew out some energy here and there, but I believe mostly they were looking for change.

F4: I just don't think he understands what we go through on a daily basis. He's a multi-billionaire. Correct me if I'm wrong, was he really ever in the working class for a long period of time?

F1: I don't know. He understands if you don't work, you don't eat. He understands that part. If you don't work, you don't eat.

F4: But I don't think he knows the daily struggles of what we're going through as working class because he's able to send his kids to college without having any worries about paying off the tuition. He doesn't have to.… I don't really know how to describe this.

F1: He worked to get there, though.

F4: Yes.

F1: He worked his butt off.

F4: Yes, but for … as for right now, he grew up during a different time. Like everyone's been saying.…

The middle classes … you're having the poor, poor, and you're having the rich, rich, but the middle class is growing smaller and smaller, and the other two are growing larger and larger and I don't think he ever really, I don't think he understands what it's like to be in that position right now.

M1: No, probably not.

F4: If that makes any sense?

F1: I'm just thinking that's he's just gone off facts, and he's just a fact person, and facts.… I don't know, you know what I mean?

I: *Say it as you're thinking it.*

F1: Well, I mean, you know how some people think, "Okay, this is this way," but if then they're only looking at facts and stuff on paper and what makes sense to them, I think.…

F4: Politics.

F1: Yes.

F2: Unfortunately, when you look at things as black or white, you miss the consequences.

F3: I agree.

F5: Yes, I agree.

F2: It's true, and there are a lot of consequences to actions when you look at things as black and white.

F1: Yes, absolutely.

F2: But I actually had this conversation with my husband the other day.

F3: There are a lot of people that follow him, though, who I think are what maybe this definition of white working class, not this white working class, but I think there are a lot that are, what makes them distinct or different, I don't know. I really don't.

F2: Personally, I think it's just that people who are die-hard republicans, and I'm republican, I'll just say, I'm definitely republican; however, there are people who are republican who will stick by him regardless of his beliefs because they're republican, and that's just wrong. Just because you're republican doesn't mean you have to back what somebody says just because they are who they are. If he's wrong, he's wrong.

F5: That's a good point.

F2: That's how I feel. Right is right and wrong is wrong. We were having this discussion the other day.

F1: The gray area is a hard place to be in.

F2: It is.

Responses to President Trump's early actions

I: *You were saying that you were having this conversation.*

F2: About some of the decisions he's making, about closing off and not allowing anybody in with visas, and banning everybody who's Iranian and Muslim.

F3: He's about to cut all the domestic violence funds by April. I just learnt this today. 100 per cent of all our items for domestic violence, so every single shelter, nothing. So, there is a lot going on.

F5: I think what the problem is with him is that he's making very quick changes. Somebody brought this up. I'm actually taking a public policy class right now in social welfare policy and what somebody said, which I think is a really good point, is that there is no grace period. He's just making very immediate changes and it's happening right now. It's happening the moment I sign this wish … in some instances it could be used, but in other instances, it's like very intimidating for people. People aren't good with change. We're seeing it a lot, happening all over the country, right now, in very negative ways, and I honestly think he's just jumping to conclusions and not looking at all his options.

F2: Well, no, it's because it's what presidents accomplish within their what, their first….

F5: 100 days.

F2: That's what he's trying to do, and unfortunately, oh my gosh, some of these things, you're right. It's boom, get this done, get this done, get this done, get this done. What are you doing? He's alienating….

F5: He literally signed the paper for the Immigration Bill as people were in flight to come here. Yes. By the time they landed….

F2: Turn around.

F5: "Well, not my problem," and then some senators and city officials lifted it temporarily and they were able to come in but it didn't hold them long.

F2: No, and he's wrong. A lot of the people come here and go to school here, or come here on work visas….

F5: Or medical.

F2: And pay high taxes, which then benefits our country and I think by making these bans, it hurts our country. Financially, it hurts our country….

F4: Higher education system.

F3: Splits families.

F2: With our education system, it hurts our country, oh my gosh, not to mention what it does to families. It hurts our country with our UN agreement. It hurts our country with treaties, it hurts our country with everything and I don't….

F5: Export, imports.

F4: Yes, well, I'm taking a race, ethnicity, and crime class this semester and doing minor and criminal justice study, so just different perspectives of different things. My instructor, she told us today that the immigration ban that Trump has put in place, there are over 9,500 students that attend ASU [Arizona State University] at this moment that are not allowed to come back. They received a letter that said you can't come back; 9,500 students that are not allowed, and that's a lot. For that teacher, for her alone, she said seven to ten of those people are in her classes, so there were, in my class alone, there were five empty seats today.

I: *So, you're seeing real tangible consequences?*

F4: We're seeing it. They were here Tuesday, or last Thursday … last Thursday, and now they're not.

F2: It's a financial hit.

F4: It is a financial hit. It is.

F1: I don't ever get into politics and this is why because once I start realizing it, it freaks me out. Not so much anymore, but it used to really freak me out and then I just work at it because it is what it is.

F3: It's overwhelming.

F5: It is overwhelming.

F1: I didn't realize all this, but then I was thinking, well maybe Trump wants everybody that's here, like, to step up. We're here. We've been born here. We have our social security number.

F2: It's scary.

F1: We're documented, you know what I mean? I get that. We've been paying taxes, we've been paying since we were born, you know what I mean? I get that. That freaked me out when I first realized that part.

F5: I think right now it's happening so rapidly and people are just reacting on Facebook, on social media, to their family.

F1: There's too much of that.

F5: And the riots, and the protests. It's like you can't keep up with it.

F2: That just makes me so mad.

F5: It becomes exhausting. There's a form of escapism that needs to happen for people because of that.

The consequences of early policy decisions

I: *What do you think is the consequence of that rapid change that's going on?*

F5: I said something similar, how we're not very good with change, right? As a society, we don't react to it well and we're seeing either two different sides of it: either people are just remaining calm and figuring out how they feel about the situation and what they want to do moving forward; and then those that are resulting in protest, or in the most extreme versions—riots, violence, hate crimes, discrimination—and it's just people, I feel, personally. I was just talking to a friend about this today; I don't know how to react to anything. I don't agree with what Trump is doing, but he's my president, but I don't agree with rioting like this because it's not going to solve anything long term.

F2: No, and it hurts people.

F5: So, what are you going to do? So, right now, I've decided that I'm going to get a master's degree in public policy and I'm going to start taking action on a legislative level and try to fight for what I believe in because it's better that I just do it now, than rely on someone else to do it, right, and it's better than rioting in the street and protesting. That's my personal opinion, though, I can't speak for everybody on that.

Race and protest

F1: The race-baiting thing is killing me, though.

F4: The what?

F1: The race thing, the race baiting, they're making it … over-publicizing all that, and it's just making it big and it's getting way out of hand, and I don't really believe that there is much of a problem with it, like, when it gets down to it.

I: *Just give me a bit more. What do you mean? A problem with what?*

F1: The news. Most of the time, they're liars.

F2: It's true.

F1: They only want you to see what they want you … you know, it's the society. It's like, "We can just throw this out there and then we can kind of get them distracted on something else where we're going to do something over here." I don't know.

I: *But what are you saying in terms of the race baiting?*

F1:	Well, I mean, there's dirt. What about the Black Lives Matter thing? I've seen this last night. I was appalled. I mean, there was this girl, there was, the F-word was every other word and she was saying, "Kill them" and "F the Whitehouse." She just showed her so-called color as what it is.
I:	*Was she black, do you mean?*
F1:	Even though she's reacting, I mean, come on? If it's going to be like this because you're a piece of work right there, everybody's going to think it. You're only making your class look like, really bad, but they're going to explode it everywhere.
I:	*Was she black?*
F1:	It was disgusting.
I:	*She was black, part of Black Lives, you mean?*
F1:	Oh yes. Yes, she was a pre-school teacher sitting there saying all this stuff. It was awful. I don't know if anybody has seen that? Oh, my gosh! I couldn't even really watch the rest of it. It was, "I'm going to teach the kids … give me all your money you white people." I mean, it was horrible. It was everywhere, though.
I:	*How did that make you feel, just listening to that?*
F1:	I was just disgusted because I don't care what color you are, but when you're going to say, "Screw me," well, screw you [laughter]!
I:	*So then it becomes divisive, does it?*
F2:	Yes, it does.
F1:	But at the same time, you do what you want to do, but just leave me out of it. Just because of the color of my skin. I don't care.
F2:	Yes, and I guess that's a very good point too. It shouldn't be anything to do with that. When it starts coming down to that, it is, it's infuriating.
F5:	It is, yes.
I:	*Anybody else on that one?*
F5:	I feel like we could go on for hours.
F4:	Yes, just move on.

Reflections and taking stock

M1:	I have something to say…. I am one of those that sits back and listens and I've taken that same stand

with the politics. In all the changes and executive orders that Trump has instituted, none of them have affected me directly and perhaps I would have a different response if they had affected me directly, but, right now, I'm just kind of sitting back and looking to see what happens because the media, the social media, it's all very inflammatory. Their purpose is to invoke emotion in us and they are going to publicize things that they know are going to invoke emotion. They're not going to report on the good things that he is doing because people are just going to sit back and say, "Ho-hum." It's not going to sell papers; it's not going to sell news time. So, I'm going to sit back and let the ripples settle a little bit because I have faith in our government and the balance of power. I know that one man does not have the ability to change every public policy and change the way this country operates within 100 days. It's not possible. … So, I'm a little bit more comfortable with the things that are going on, just because I know that things are going to level out. He's probably trying to get some momentum started in showing that he is going to be aggressive but I think that's all it is right now.

I: *So, he's playing politics?*

M1: Yes, and I think he's probably got a lot of people behind him that are telling him, "You need to do this now. You need to get started now because this is what you told the American public you were going to do, so get into office and start showing that you're doing something."

F1: The way that he's backing all the police officers and all that, you know? I like that part. You do what you've got to do because, before, it was that time where it was just about all the hatred that was going on. That was very infuriating. I'm sure for you too.

F2: Oh, yes.

Communities coming together

I: *That's great, thank you for that. Just thinking about different communities, how do people that are different come together?*

	Different people, so, different ethnicities, classes, do they come together and where do they come together?
F1:	Church.
F2:	Absolutely.
F4:	I feel like the last time I remember that I saw unity across not just Phoenix, but across the whole nation, was when 9/11 happened, the only other time I've ever seen our country as unified.
F2:	In tragedy.
F5:	In tragedy, I was going to say that too.
F4:	Tragedy I think is really the only time that we're actually going to come together and put our differences aside to come together and work together. But I also don't have experience of anything else except for tragedy bringing people together.

Feel-good stories connect people

F5:	Well, there are other aspects. You can bring out more joyous circumstances. I mean, especially with social media the way it is. I hate to bring it up because it's very superficial, but, like, I'm going to do it anyway. This whole "Beyoncé is having twins," thing. People are freaking out about it. All socio-economic statuses, all ages, it's a real thing and people are freaking out about it.
M2:	My age? I don't even know … well, I know who Beyoncé is, but….
F3:	The Kardashians?
F5:	I know. But it's true and, like, some people said it's a form of escapism with the political climate and that it plays a role in it, but I think more joyous circumstances do that too. Sometimes take us by surprise, Chewbacca mum, is another big one. We all know who that is, and I brought her up, right?
F3:	I just love you.
F2:	No, you're right.
I:	*Chewbacca?*
F5:	I'm trying to lighten the mood in this joint after that conversation [laughter].
I:	*What's Chewbacca mum? Is that out of Star Wars, Chewbacca?*

F4: I don't know either, so you're good.

F5: She put on a Chewbacca mask and laughed a lot and she ended up on Ellen.

M1: It was a mother who did a Facebook video and she had just bought this little Chewbacca mask and she videotaped herself in the car just laughing hysterically. It went viral.

F5: I'm not saying it's important, but a lot of people watched it and a lot of people enjoyed it. It made you feel good and then everybody watched her on Ellen, and guess what, they felt good.

Connecting across differences locally

I: *I think that's a really important point, actually. What about locally?*

M1: Community. When you said that, I thought of community events. Before Christmas, we had a public safety event and all the police department, the Peoria police department, got together and the fire department and there were all kinds of booths and it was at a big community park and we had all kinds of people. So, everybody in that area, people started getting together, and kids playing games, those types of events.

I: *What about sports events? Because sport is a big thing?*

F5: Superbowl, I guess.

F2: Yes, that's true too.

F4: Football games. They get together for football or commercials.

F5: Sporting events, yes.

I: *Do you think city government represents local residents?*

F2: I don't see them as a presence. At least for where I live, I don't see them coming to places where we live.

M1: I wouldn't know who they are. My city government, I wouldn't know who they are by face.

F5: That's a very good point.

F2: Well, we wouldn't know them necessarily by face, but they do a really good job here in our municipality, when you talk about our parks.

M1: From what I see, yes.

F2: Yes, I mean, they do a really good job. So, I think our city government and especially when you think about all they do as we have a lot of stuff they do in the city over at the park.

F5: At the mall parks and stuff.

F2: The Aquatics Centre and mall parks, so I would say, for our city, absolutely.

I: *Just for the record, when we're saying "our city" we mean Surprise, we don't mean the big metropolitan?*

F5: Directly where we're at now, yes.

F2: Just the city, I mean, the city of Phoenix, they have the First Fridays. They do a lot of craft things downtown all the time.

I: *The people in charge, though, do you feel they have a presence?*

F5: I feel like they help administer things but I feel like they're not getting, I mean, they're not on the ground. Like he said, I couldn't point them out if I saw them. I work at a grocery store, I couldn't point them out if I saw them walk in there.

F3: But the Mayor as a figurehead, he'll come and speak to a breakfast luncheon or get up in the front of the press but then as you....

F2: There's no way. You would have to really make yourself known to them to know who they are to be able to see them. There's no way.

I: *What about communities that are, then, separated, or even segregated? How would you bring such communities together?*

F1: The other side of the tracks [laughter].

F4: Volunteering.

M1: It would have to be some event that was very highly publicized across all different types of media sources, and an incentive for all ages to attend. For instance, I think about a long time ago when I worked in downtown Phoenix, as a police officer, we had the Fourth July event and it was way down at the capital and they would have a venue of all kinds of different artists to come and do a concert, and they had fireworks and all kinds of different things represented and they would advertise it and the whole entire capital mall would just be filled with people. People from all over, across the valley would come to see that event but it would have to be communicated really well to get across to, you know, that vast expanse. The city government would have to do that....

We have certain churches in this area that have campuses in different cities. We have one church called the Christchurch of the Valley and they have campuses in a lot of different cities. They could, essentially, get some type of event and communicate it because they're a large entity, they'd have that ability to communicate and connect all different types of communities, from Peoria, to Avondale, to Surprise.

F2: Our elementary school is also very involved with the families in the neighborhood. They have a "come watch the stars" astronomy night. They had a magic show that was, like, mum-and-son night. Come watch the magic show, and dinner.... Fall festivals, dancing, when the parents come.

M1: I think a lot of schools across the valley do those kinds of things.... They figure if they energize the children, the children are going to go home and say, "Hey, mum and dad, I want to go to this."

F2: Yes, and it works.

M1: It works because the children are persistent.

F2: I mean, they have all the food trucks lining the parking lots, and the magicians come and whatever.

I: *Okay, is there anything else you want to say?*

F3: Where did your interest come in doing this?

F4: I do have a question for you because I'm a little incompetent with this situation, but how do our politics affect the UK? Like, with Donald Trump getting in, how does that affect you guys or in Europe, or anything like that?

I: *I can answer those. Is there anything directly in terms of the research? Well, thank you very much everybody.*

Conclusion

This focused discussion took place in a home outside of Phoenix, Arizona, soon after the inauguration of the new president in 2017. It aims to put the reader in the place of both the researcher and the

Empathy

participants as the conversation developed. While it has been edited and the names taken out, it follows the flow of the discussion as it occurred. The reader will make their own interpretations of the data but we were focused on claims of believability (Wellman, 1977) by showcasing one near-complete transcript from many interviews and interactions as part of an exploratory research.

The discussion offers an insight into how familiarity, belonging, safety, place, space, and change are key markers for how we position ourselves in relation to others. People and community loom large through the lens of family, location, and class. As illustrated in earlier chapters, race and certainly "white" as a category of meaning and experience was often not talked about. The meaning of working class was contested. The sense of diversity in their neighborhoods was sometimes overstated and contradicted, and in other experiences, was seen as ordinary. Racialized neighborhoods were elsewhere, where there were differences, social problems, and needs.

The new President was a divisive figure in the discussions. Support for Trump was not overwhelming, but he was seen as a change candidate. The disruption being witnessed on the ground was seen negatively. The new President was seen as making rapid changes that were having direct, real-life consequences. The President's focus on holding binary positions was seen as avoiding complexity and without nuance. "White" as an identity emerged through the actions and experiences of "black" people and the lived experiences of differences and diversity. Claiming to live in a racially and ethnically diverse area was challenged. Was it enough to say that an area is diverse if there are one or two racially and ethnically diverse families?

The discussion highlighted how living away from the sprawling city of Phoenix provides benefits to all the participants, including reciprocity, local connections, and a sense of home. However, if you want to consume and experience diversity and difference as an everyday reality, you have to let others organize it, seek it out, or consider moving out of the area you grew up in. Identity, belonging, and experiencing differences and diversity are fluid processes, as much a personal choice as a structural and cultural condition.

6

The challenges of cross-racial coalition building

Introduction

The chapter will look forward to consider the possibilities of building cross-racial coalitions between the white working class and communities of color as the US transitions from majority white to a minority white country. In doing so, it will state that 50 years after the campaign for civil rights and the passage of landmark legislation during the 1960s, there is little evidence of formal and sustainable cross-racial coalition building at the grassroots or grasstops level between the white working class and communities of color. White working-class communities wanted to engage with communities of color but did not have the means of engaging across racial boundaries beyond a superficial everyday level. Discussions between different communities were "soft-wired" and based on fleeting exchanges in informal spaces rather than becoming "hard-wired" in a strategic plan that can create a framework for coalition building. Stakeholders were largely ambivalent and occasionally hostile toward engaging with white working-class communities to build effective cross-racial alliances. Similar to white working-class communities in relation to communities of color, stakeholders found it challenging to engage with these groups.

White working-class communities are racially diverse

Our study demonstrated that the lived experiences of white working-class communities created opportunities to engage with communities of color in workplaces, schools, and neighborhoods. They may feel disconnected from political representatives and left behind in terms of opportunities for economic advancement, but many spoke in positive ways about being part of racially diverse families and neighborhoods.

In resident-based focus groups, discussions often touched on racial diversity within the personal lives of white working-class people. In doing so, participants complicated the notion of the uniformity of white working-class communities by referencing their own family membership. Some viewed themselves through the prism of racial hybridity, which was sometimes deployed to absolve themselves from the charge of being racist:

> 'As far as white and black, we have a big white population, a big Hispanic population, a big mixed. A lot of our kids are mixed, which is nice in a way because when people talk about the working class being racists, it's like a lot of them have at least, have mixed children and then it kind of makes the grandparents follow.' (Dayton FG)

According to this participant increased levels of racial hybridity may help to break down common-sense racist views of older white people toward communities of color. Similarly, the following person displayed equal amounts of affection toward his grandchildren whether they were Asian-, Irish-, or Italian-American, with the inference being that claims of racism would appear to be irrational: "*I have two grandchildren that are half-American, half-Asiatic. I have a daughter-in-law that's Asiatic. Wonderful family. Wonderful daughter-in-law. And I love those kids as much as I loved … the other ones that are Italian/Irish*" (Bay Ridge FG).

Yet, having racial hybridity within families was also more than a mechanism to avoid or absolve difficult conversations about racism; it also forced many white working-class families to confront the realities of racism in intimate and painful ways. Some of our participants discussed the problems of having racist family members and, at the same time, having people of color for whom they have a strong personal affection:

> 'My father is completely and totally racist.… I've got a sister who is with a black man right now, and has a mixed child. He would not let her step foot in that house for the whole first year of her life because of who her father was. Does he love her? Yes.… I get those dirty looks when I'm at Wal-Mart with my niece, does that make me love her less when people automatically assume that she's my child because she looks a lot like me? No, I own that. Yeah, she's mine, for the time being. Do I tell them, "This is just my niece? I'm sorry, she's half-black, whatever?" No.' (Birmingham FG)

Initially, there is acceptance of the reality of racism in white working-class families, with an outright rejection of racial diversity in the family. In time, the racist father grows to love his granddaughter in the personal space of the home after coming to terms with the decision of his child to be in a relationship with a person of color. The participant also recounts the everyday and direct racism experienced in everyday situations when with her niece.

Awareness of race and racism

White working-class communities are commonly viewed as supporters of extremist and nationalist positions such as those highlighted by the media during the 2016 presidential campaign of Donald Trump. In contrast to this perspective, the experiences of those who participated in the study were different because they had greater contact with communities of color than some who could afford to live in more middle-class neighborhoods. This meant that our participants had greater awareness of the impact of racism. For example, a participant explained that having an Asian-American wife had educated him about racial discrimination, which would not have otherwise been the case. Indeed, the issues of race and racism were raised frequently in discussions that took place in the midst of the 2016 presidential election. People were very concerned about the racist overtones and anti-immigrant rhetoric:

> 'I have children that are Hispanic and then there's my husband's family, who are immigrants from Africa and who are also Muslim. So, there's a lot of feelings going around in my house right now. My children are worried about their grandparents being deported. My husband's worrying about his family, who are actually visiting home right now, whether they're going to be able to get back into the country because they're a Muslim, and they're immigrants. So, I feel right now, it's, it's a lot of uncertainty. The best thing that we can do is just come together.' (Phoenix FG)

The close familial and diverse relationships show that white working-class communities are enmeshed in the immigration policies implemented since 2016, which includes a ban of people travelling to the US from Muslim-majority countries, the increased and intense vetting of arrivals to the US, and executive orders to build a wall on the southern border with Mexico (Pierce et al, 2018). The reality of these changes is played out in fears of grandparents being separated from children, and the concerns of adult children about whether parents will be allowed back to the US.

Diverse friendship networks

Countering the view of white working-class communities as being hostile toward people of color, there were numerous examples of participants sharing experiences of racially diverse friendship networks and how this should be viewed as normal rather than the exception:

> 'I live with a Muslim and a lesbian, and I'm a straight white male.' (Birmingham FG)
>
> 'My dad was a steelworker and his best friend was a black man.' (Birmingham FG)
>
> 'I think I have one friend, two friends, out of my whole entire, everyone that I talk to, that I am close to, that are white. Everybody else has some kind of different ethnicity, race, and some kind of different background to myself.' (Phoenix FG)

The experience of valuing diversity in working-class communities was seen as more commonplace among millennials and Generation Z, namely, those born in the 1980s and afterwards: "*my grandchildren they have black friends, they have Asian friends*" (Tacoma FG); "*Each other's kids, it doesn't, their version of race won't be the same, they don't see it, they don't think about it*" (Birmingham FG).

Many participants were optimistic about race relations improving because of the way in which young people view diversity as being a normalized part of their lived experiences. On many occasions, the people engaged in discussions were reluctant to make specific reference to the ethnicity of their friends, often preferring color-blind language—speaking in a way that treats everyone the same—as the best way of addressing racism. In the following quote the erasure of race is shown: "*I have a 40-year Hispanic friend who has been one of my best friends for that long. And quite frankly, at this point, you would have to point out that he's Hispanic to me because he's X*" (Tacoma FG). Another participant in his 50s spoke about growing up in a diverse neighborhood with friends who were Irish, German, Hispanic, Italian, and black. They shared meals in one another's homes: "*You know, I'm not going to say, but my friends that were Irish, German, Hispanic and black, 'Oh, let's go over Dominic's house and eat, his mother's a good cook', you know, would cook, it didn't matter*" (Bay Ridge FG).

These experiences created a platform to understand each other in an informal way without having this implemented in a "forced" manner. Across all case-study sites, and similar to being part of a racially diverse family, being part of a mixed friendship network was also claimed as evidence of not being a racist and of change. When the question was posed: "*What do you think of the view that white working-class people are racist?*", the response from a participant was unequivocal, "*I think it's a lie.*" This person continues to provide further evidence to back up this response by pointing to the camaraderie between her father and his colleagues in the police force, where people had to rely on each other: "*My father was a white male police officer who had two … best female friends who were black female police officers.… I mean, they were at our house a lot growing up, it was not odd for us in any way, shape, or form*" (Birmingham FG).

Neighborhood diversity as commonplace

Racial and ethnic diversity is part of neighborhood life for many white working-class people. Participants described living in close proximity to immigrants and people of color, as well as interacting with diverse people as neighbors, at the playground, and through informal conversations. This was a normalized experience that they suggest challenges the common-sense and stereotypical imagery of white working-class communities as being racist:

> 'I grew up in a diverse neighborhood, right. I still have the childhood friend, Frankie; he calls me "brother," okay, when he was the only Chinese man in the neighborhood.… I still have Puerto Rican friends, alright.' (Bay Ridge FG)

> 'There's three black families on my street, and our school is probably 50 per cent black.' (Birmingham FG)

> 'This is a very culturally diverse neighborhood. I won't mention names; we have somebody born in Brazil, we've got a couple of Puerto Ricans, we've got one from El Salvador, we've got the African-American family and their extended family moved in. And then we've got a couple of whites.' (Phoenix FG)

In Bay Ridge, participants talked about hosting a Christmas Eve dinner for neighbors of different backgrounds. They come together, interact, and share food with each other.

The participants generally characterize the diversity in their neighborhoods as a good thing and put forward that "*We are a melting pot*." One person explained that there were many Muslim people living nearby and that they "*all get along*." Another participant stated that she reached out to a Muslim woman with young children to tell them about local resources. However, set against those who embraced the changes were also others who were more hostile:

> 'The neighborhood has changed quite a bit since I was a youth. You know, it was very much a, it's always been a working-class neighborhood: Italians, Irish, Scandinavians, Greeks. For the last 30 years or so, we've had some, some Muslims, some Asians, you know. East Asians come in, and it's been interesting to see the changing of the neighborhood. I embrace it; I know that, you know, America is a nation of immigrants. Some people are not in agreement with me, even some of my friends. You know, I know people personally who are going to be voting for Trump this year, much to my dismay.... But, yes, no I think, I think it's great for the neighborhood. I think it helps to open up people's minds, even unwillingly, in some cases.' (Bay Ridge FG)

Rejecting neighborhood diversity

Some believed that those who do not like the diversity just keep to themselves. Others felt that people moved away from the neighborhood if they did not like the demographic changes occurring: "*I think the open-minded people are the ones that stayed. You just work together*" (Phoenix FG). We saw similar judgments toward those who did not like neighborhood diversity. In Dayton, a focus group participant criticized those white working-class neighbors with "unwelcoming attitudes" just because a new neighbor was from a different country, or because they let their kids play in the yard.

Embracing diversity as ongoing change

Often, the acceptance of diversity is rooted in a neighborhood's immigrant history, being part of its identity:

> 'We've seen a lot of changes, a lot of changing faces.... Some for the good, some for the bad.... And this neighborhood was founded on diversity ... the fabric of this community in itself was founded between our German families ... and then there was the Appalachian kids.... I think the community, why it is more acceptable, is because we came from all those immigrants.' (Dayton FG)

The appreciation of racial and ethnic diversity, particularly immigrants, was also directly related to the physical transformation and economic impacts of immigrants moving in. Focus group participants mentioned the revitalization of neighborhoods, commercial corridors, and even churches as something positive about the changes they saw taking place:

> 'We started to lose our congregation. But then what happened was, all of a sudden, we started getting Russian people moving here, Polish people, Spanish people, Mexican, people from Ecuador, and now the parish has a Spanish mass on Saturday and Sunday because it's starting, our faith is starting to grow again.' (Bay Ridge FG)

> 'I think that they are the most fantastic residents that we have had because they take such great pride in everything that they own. I've seen then transform house after house in the community that have been vacant, abandoned in this neighborhood.' (Dayton FG)

> 'You can tell when Hispanics live next to you ... it has a nice pink house and across the road is green. Back in the days when I came here, we had police officers, doctors, and nurses. Where are they now? You don't see them ... you see the nice landscaping, the nice pink house, so you see a diversion.' (Phoenix FG)

Diverse relationships are not hard-wired

There was evidence of white working-class people interviewed in the focus groups valuing the importance of difference among family, friends, work colleagues, and neighbors. They expressed interest in the everyday lived experience of diversity and making it work. In fact, across 415 interviews, there were few who were actively hostile about diversity, race, and immigration. Many white working-class people that we met responded in the positive, but they also used color-blind language, and other racialized tropes that people of color would find offensive. Additionally, we found that support for diversity was mostly superficial once you got outside the circle of the family. Many interactions occurred in the street, in shops, or over the yard fence, but these did not lead to intimate and deep friendships, or profound changes in the order of things. In some instances, contact was avoided altogether, with diversity seen as a threat: "*When I drive downtown, I keep a gun in my lap*" (Birmingham FG).

We heard a desire to get to know new immigrant neighbors more than actual examples of people getting to know them. One participant from Dayton said that she welcomed immigrants living on her street but that she had yet to form friendships with any of them. Focus group participants did react when asked about the limits of living in a diverse neighborhood. In one focus group, we asked what they would do if black or Turkish families invited them to come over to their house:

> 'I would not go.... They don't speak English, and second of all, if a black person ... probably has like grudges or something and that's going to be awkward. And then ... you don't know who's got bedbugs or what you're bringing home with you. Like, I'm super-strict, I give you like a look down before you walk into the doors, and I'm like "I don't know about you."' (Dayton FG)

In other focus groups, we heard descriptions of white working-class people sticking together and not connecting with non-white neighbors. One Bay Ridge participant described the behavior and attitudes of the white working class as "*clan like*," and in Phoenix, a focus group participant described her neighborhood as "*cliquey*" despite its perceived diversity. Even in those areas perceived as diverse neighborhoods, it was pointed out that not all of the streets are diverse: "*We are all white on our street and we're all white on the street next door*" (Phoenix FG).

The changing demographics in neighborhoods, and the corresponding impacts on social, cultural, and economic dynamics, stimulated more racially charged conversations: "*When I bought my house ... I didn't tell too many people I was buying a house over here. When I told one guy, he said he had friends that lived over here but because of all these Mexican people moving over here, they ended up moving north*" (Phoenix FG). Here, a woman does not want to tell people where she lives because the neighborhood is viewed as undesirable by white people. In this case, the mere presence of Mexicans signals to white people that a neighborhood is on the decline and there is reason to move out.

Perceptions of segregation

In many focus groups, we challenged the participants about the characterization of their neighborhood. We asked if they lived in a racially segregated neighborhood. Discussions about segregation were difficult at times because some denied its existence, at least where they lived. In one focus group in Birmingham, when we asked: "*Hold on for a second, Birmingham, 75 per cent black, and the outlying areas are largely white, is that not a definition of racial segregation?*", the response was: "*No.... Now there are certain areas where all black or all white, and you would kind of be an outcast, or an outsider if you moved in.*" (Birmingham FG)

Similar to having a black friend as evidence of not being a racist, focus group participants did not think of mostly homogeneous white neighborhoods as segregated. The presence of some racial and ethnic diversity was evidence of not being segregated.

At times, participants used language that many would find offensive, particularly people of color. As mentioned earlier, race was mostly talked about indirectly, in coded and color-blind ways. This is not simply a white working-class phenomenon, but a white one. For example, we heard comments such as: "*We don't really see race as a thing here*" (Tacoma FG); "*They're just like us*" (Dayton FG); "*I don't really see the race*" (Phoenix FG); and "*My kids don't see color*" (Birmingham FG). In part, these comments illustrate how the study participants were grappling with the changing make-up of their communities. They were looking for commonalities—ways to connect and reduce distance between themselves and others who look different—but they did not understand how such comments increased distance by denying racism and racial differences.

Denial of racism

Sometimes, those involved in trying to bring people of different backgrounds together did not see that racism acted through, for example, police and community relations, and had a detrimental impact on black and minority ethnic communities. The denial of racism or its severity came up in a discussion about Black Lives Matter. Several Bay Ridge focus groups debated the legitimacy of the movement. Some saw the protests as undermining police power. They argued that if African-Americans just showed more respect to police officers, they could avoid the problem of police brutality. One person commented: "*All lives matter.*" Another could not understand how a police officer could be the "*bad guy*" when the police were the ones stopping criminals. In a different focus group in Bay Ridge, white working-class participants supported Black Lives Matter. They believed that African-Americans were "*treated like crap.*" This same person also stated that everyone should be treated as equals.

It was not uncommon for some participants to see racism as less serious than in the past, or as less overt than before. Some participants felt that making racial jokes was not being racist. Some thought that people of color were too sensitive. Others were tired of what they perceived as political correctness. Another focus group in the same community saw things entirely differently. One young woman, who works with mostly white men in the trades, identified some of her co-workers as more outwardly racist. They used "*the N-word,*" discredited the work of African-American tradesmen, and blasted out Trump speeches in the workplace. This participant had spoken out against this explicit racism in her work: "*I've literally told someone to shut the f**k up during lunch break*" (Dayton FG).

Those who understand institutional racism and white privilege could move beyond the interpersonal interactions and see the systemic nature of racial inequality. One participant from Bay Ridge shared a personal story of his friend from Tobago, who was excluded from work functions while white employees were not. This member fought against his friend's exclusion and felt that he understood prejudice because of this relationship. We heard similar stories in our other sites:

> 'I never thought about it, but my background was employment, helping people and work. And having worked at various locations throughout the Phoenix area, I notice the difference in how white people get hired easily.... A lot of the minorities I dealt with, they were willing to take just about anything. Whereas the white people, they're more specific.' (Phoenix FG)

Here, this participant describes seeing how race influenced who gets hired for which jobs. Additionally, he saw that white jobseekers could be pickier because they had more jobs to choose from compared with people of color.

The challenges to cross-racial coalition building

Given this landscape of white working-class people living among diverse people, living separate lives, lacking awareness of white privilege, and using color-blind thinking, how do people of different races and ethnicities come together? How are white working-class people building a future with working-class communities of color? When we asked focus group participants to describe instances where they came together with people of different races and ethnic backgrounds, most paused. This question stumped participants. It was hard to come up with examples of cross-racial connections. We met a handful of white working-class people who were community organizers actively trying to bridge divides between communities. In most cases, these interventions were more at the idea stage and required investment and time to have an opportunity of succeeding. The focus groups' discussions usually centered on potential rather than actual instances, such as the need for community spaces and events, as well as advice on how to get the conversation started.

The few examples of coalition building were at an embryonic stage of just learning how to communicate and resolve immediate and small neighborhood-level challenges. In Phoenix, we learned about a neighborhood conflict around parking cars on the front lawn. The neighborhood organizers, who were white and working class, spent time talking with the new residents, mostly Mexican immigrants, who were parking in ways that the white residents could not comprehend. Taking a friendly approach, that is, not confrontational or involving the police, worked and the neighborhood no longer has cars parked on the lawns:

> 'Rather than hostile, "You dirty so and so. Why don't you park on the street like everybody else?" ... so, we certainly had our culture conflicts. And the language barrier ... the fear of police.... So, we've had to make some adaptations and acknowledgments that these people didn't have the life we grew up with, they didn't live here and the truth is they're here now and we need them as much as anybody else to be a part of our community and participate. And they're going to come a little bit our way; we've got to go a little bit their way to make that work, and anything less than that actually is unacceptable. The community is what it is and you've got to make it work; failure is not an option.' (Phoenix FG)

While a seemingly simple example, this recounting shows the challenges that residents face in getting to know their neighbors and agreeing neighborhood norms. These neighborhood organizers wanted people to get along, so they chose to engage their new neighbors in ways that allowed for future interactions.

While not explicitly stated in the earlier Phoenix example, showing "respect" and "tolerance" came up as key ingredients for bringing people together in our other sites. As one person succinctly put it: "*when you're tolerant to somebody, they have to be tolerant of you*" (Bay Ridge FG). In Tacoma, we learned about the process of getting neighborhood residents engaged around a site for a potential playground. Neighborhood organizers convened activities to create new neighborhood traditions. Once the county government saw the enthusiasm and participation of residents, they installed the equipment:

> 'With the construction of our playground, I think that's how we got, we became successful, because even before the playground, we were having events at that plot, you know, like every season, we have an Easter egg hunt and it went from zero people to 150 people from the community to show it was pretty amazing, and that's when the county recognized, "Hey, we need to give them a park." But we basically not only built a park, we built a community, we built a tradition that every season, we can have something here.' (Tacoma FG)

In Dayton, we learned of street-level interactions to improve the neighborhood. Although they seem small, the neighborhood leaders are clearly laying the groundwork for more ambitious efforts. One neighborhood group organized a clean-up event for a local park. The neighborhood organizers—two white working-class men—approached the park users to help, in this case, Spanish-speaking immigrants who play soccer at the park:

> 'We went up there because we were going to a parks project, we just wanted to address it to them and see if they would help. I just asked for their time and if they had it, a financial contribution doing a fundraiser. Over two weekends, 50 of them showed up—31 one weekend, 20 the other—and we did four hours of work, intensive, manual labor over both weekends. I asked myself "Why are they here?" Well, they feel a sense of community and ownership, pride all in that one space.' (Dayton FG)

Reflecting on the initial interaction, one of the neighborhood organizers said he was nervous to approach the men playing soccer because he did not speak Spanish and was not sure how the men would react. He expected some hostility or disinterest. The positive interaction motivated him to reach out more. Now the soccer games are drawing in others from the neighborhood.

Except for a few organizations that are dealing with neighborhood improvement, crime, and poverty in diverse neighborhoods, it was generally agreed that cross-racial coalition building is not happening. It is still a struggle for those groups as well. Getting people to occupy the same space and then to work together for a common cause is fraught with challenges.

Everyday and organized interactions

People did come together in everyday activities and for special events, for example, parades, festivals, shopping, and sporting events. Some participants viewed local festivals and activities as a positive preliminary measure to forming community cohesion. Food, soccer, and music all came up as activities that attract a diverse group of people: "*People don't come together on their own yet, but they come together when there's any kind of a gathering event*" (Dayton FG). For example, participants rattled off the names of local events where a diverse range of people already come together: "*Adventure Night*" (Dayton FG); "*First Friday*" (Phoenix FG); "*70s Soul Revival*" (Tacoma FG); "*Arts Walk*" (Birmingham FG); and "*Summer Stroll*" (Bay Ridge FG). Other examples included sporting events, church-related activities, the arts, and volunteering. Building on what we already saw happening in practice, focus group participants suggested more localized neighborhood events and spaces for coming together, such as block parties, community gardens, and play groups:

> 'I think in the long term, more localized events need to happen because it will allow you to create that neighbor to neighbor, but the thing is most neighborhoods aren't organized well enough to do it.' (Dayton FG)

> 'Maybe if there was some, like, unified community event, then we could all come together.' (Birmingham FG)

> 'The block party, what I like about it is, I go out and I give out the flyers. I say, "Oh you just moved in? … Someone across the street has three kids your age, really." I said, "Yes,

> yes, you will meet them at the block party." I think it's important.' (Bay Ridge FG)

Another member of this group explained that because her neighborhood did not have a block party, they used the marathon that comes down their street as a way to get together. She explained that schools represent spaces for diverse people to come together. However, a few people, and definitely not the consensus across our sites, felt that coalition building should be more explicitly political. The focus for these participants was about community organizing for social change: getting people to attend marches in addition to "*breaking bread together*" (Bay Ridge FG). The point here was really to get people talking, sharing their lives, and learning about the complexities of living in a racist society: "*My idea was we need to have a bunch of people in the community, marching through the community to show that, yes … we do support.*" Striving to build common space, such as a community centre, was one idea that galvanized some people that we spoke with during our work. In Birmingham, they suggested locations that were "in-between" in order to bridge the divide between white and black neighborhoods.

Diverse community representations needed

Additionally, to really see cross-racial coalition building happening, more diverse community representation was required in, for example, parent–teacher associations (PTAs) and community boards. For that to happen, translation services would also need to be offered. With more engagement, perhaps social cohesion could inspire coalition building. White working-class people are unable to communicate with working-class people of color beyond the friendly "hello," and even this is challenged by physical separation in some cases. Of course, there are close family connections and friendships, but in terms of spurring cross-racial coalition building, focus group participants came up with a variety of explanations for the lack of cross-racial dialogue, including lack of interest, language barriers, and racial tension.

One woman from Bay Ridge described her experience of trying to get to know different people in her building:

> 'The trouble is, they don't want to interact … even though I say where I live … I'm friendly with everybody in my building.… But there's some that close the door right in my face.… They don't want to be friends. You try so hard.…

> Talk, "hello," "good luck," they'll close the door right in my face and have. And do I get upset? No, I go, "What am I going to do?" But I feel bad.... It's just that they don't want to.' (Bay Ridge FG)

Some talked about really not knowing how to bring people together and speculated that even well-intentioned efforts could be viewed as intrusive. One focus group participant recognized the need to do outreach but also wondered if some burden should be placed on African-Americans for not showing up: "*there's very, very few African-Americans participate. And I haven't seen a lot of outreach, but then on the other side is 'Where are you? Where are you?'*" (Tacoma FG).

Others talked about hosting neighborhood socials with outreach to all the residents in the neighborhood. However, few immigrants or African-Americans ever attend. In one case, it was possibly because the events take place at a local Christian church, which might not be a comfortable meeting place. Interestingly, this same focus group also noted that white working class people hardly talk to the non-white people who attend: "*The Hispanic groups ... they will engage with a lot of people. But the other minorities are actually, they've started to just not accept invitations to different things because they get invited but no one talks to them*" (Dayton FG).

In some cases, there were practical reasons why it was hard to bring people together, namely, language barriers. Some found it difficult to converse through translators, often children. However, in one focus group, a participant expressed interest in learning Spanish so that she could better communicate with neighbors: "*About a month ago, I discussed buying one of those voice recorders that translates.... And start carrying it around. We have to change, so let's change for the better. There's ways to figure it out. They are just like us*" (Dayton FG).

Overcoming barriers and expectations

Some expressed embarrassment at perceived cultural misunderstandings. For example, some participants felt that they should not have to learn the language of newcomers; rather, immigrants should learn English. Finally, segregation, racial tension, and distrust cast a big shadow over these communities. We spoke with many engaging people who seemed genuinely interested in bringing people together, but the larger community context was rife with unresolved racial conflict and considerable wariness about people's true intentions. The presidential campaign and election of Trump only worsened existing challenges.

Instances where people could come together and build bridges had been quickly squelched: "*A woman was stabbed and hospitalized who was Mexican in our neighborhood. I spoke up on our neighborhood board and I got shot down*" (Phoenix FG). Another participant put the issue about immigrants and white working-class residents more bluntly: "*They don't trust us, we don't trust them*" (Dayton FG).

We heard similar types of assertions made elsewhere: "*It's just so deeply rooted because of our history here, Birmingham. Just mistrust, like black people just do not trust white people here. Even thinking about, like, some of my millennial friends, like, they don't even trust black people*" (Birmingham FG). Here, focus group participants suggest that the police would need to be present to have an event that brought people together. People would not be willing to risk their lives without security.

Cross-racial coalition building: perspectives from key informants

The prospects for cross-racial coalition building are not on the immediate agenda of most of the key informants that we interviewed. Similar to what we heard in the resident focus groups, key informants also pointed out the importance of food- and culture-based festivals as a way to get people of different racial and ethnic backgrounds to interact. However, after that, key informants struggled to come up with ways that institutions and organizations were intentionally bringing working-class people of different backgrounds together beyond entertainment.

Key informants involved in community organizing were able to give some examples of diverse people coming together around immigration rights and racial justice, but it was unclear whether white working-class people were the ones participating. Most of the examples of cross-racial coalition building were informal and small in scale. Key informants believed that this was the way to break down prejudice. Across the sites, key informants emphasized youth as being more open to diversity. Public schools were pointed to as the place where mixing and working together naturally happens: "*I think young people are very much more open to that, that's the impression I've gotten, actually*" (Phoenix KI).

One key informant from Dayton spoke about a program where immigrants are invited to share their stories. This informant witnessed at first hand how dialogue can reduce prejudice. Furthermore, the high school brings small groups of native-born and immigrant students together to take trips to museums, performances, and sports events.

The program had built strong relationships among the students and families. The director of the program has witnessed these native-born white working-class children standing up against prejudice in the school (Dayton KI).

Overall, key informants found bringing people together to be fraught with difficulties and expressed a fair bit of skepticism about cross-racial coalition building: "*Unfortunately, I don't think it's happening enough outside of the educational context and I think when it does, it's more rhetoric than anything*" (Birmingham KI). Many pointed to the problem of segregated neighborhoods and segregated lives, even in diverse New York City: "*There's an imagination that in New York City, because of the diversity, everyone is just friends with each other but there's not. There's usually communities who are living next to each other but they don't interact with each other*" (Bay Ridge KI). It seemed challenging for organizers and communities to get people together and to have honest conversations about neighborhood issues, let alone tackle complex issues about racism, privilege, and inequality:

> 'My hope would be, yes, and that, like, we talk about that. We are very honest with folks but … people in this program are going to be coming from a variety of different backgrounds and that's going to be hard. We're basically setting ourselves up for conflict and setting ourselves up for difficult conversations because that's not something that we often will, kind of, locate ourselves within.' (Phoenix KI)

As conversations can get heated, white communities are hesitant to move beyond the superficial and unable to see other perspectives. Even those trained in racial awareness and white privilege felt unprepared:

> 'I think that we fail. We still fail to figure out what … where our common ground is … with poor and working-class communities of color. We still have not figured out the clear, concise way to just beat it over people's heads that there are intersections of interest that the same forces that are holding down, you know, poor and white, poor and working class.… I know I'm not capable of doing that.' (Bay Ridge KI)

In conclusion, conversations with key informants are consistent with what we heard from white working-class residents. Few organizations, either governmental or non-profit, are working at bringing diverse working-class people together. Most of those efforts to do so do not engage white working-class people. The few initiatives that exist are small and informal. Those working on such coalition building lack capacity and need support.

Conclusion

This chapter investigated the prospects of cross-racial coalition building between white working-class communities and communities of color. More than 50 years after the success of the civil rights movement in leading to landmark legislation regarding equality of opportunity, we found few concrete examples of people coming together across racial boundaries. This may or may not be surprising given the legacy of race and racism in the US.

Often, white working-class communities have been pitted against communities of color within a framework embedded in conflict and resentment. The view has been taken that the former is a stumbling block to progress because they are generally perceived to hold racialized views and are against any form of racial justice. Indeed, some stakeholders across all of our case-study sites demonstrated these concerns to explain the lack of progress on coalition building. They did not see white working-class communities as key building blocks and generally did not have the know-how to engage with these groups. Yet, the white working-class residents that we met were sometimes far removed from this stereotype. They spoke fondly about diversity within their own family and having close friends who were people of color. Often, this was used to counter the claims of racism leveled at white working-class communities. However, similar in a way to stakeholders' lack of skills in engaging with them, they too did not have the confidence or awareness for meaningful interactions with communities of color. In the event that there was any cross-racial coalition building, this was very much fleeting and "soft-wired" rather than sustained and "hard-wired."

Given the febrile nature of race and politics in the US that we witnessed during our research and the subsequent way in which discussion has been shaped since, there is an urgent need for foundations and public sector organizations to review the way in which they engage with white working-class communities. In doing so, there may be the prospect of the type of innovative coalition building required from the ground up that could be sustained in the long term and change the way communities are perceived.

7

Conclusion

Introduction

We focused on exploring the views and lived experiences of white working-class people regarding how they define and see the white working class, race, and change, the challenges of selecting a president, and the opportunities for building cross-racial coalitions at a local level. Our analysis has been grounded on primary data from 415 interviews across five different locations in the US, namely: New York City, Birmingham, AL; Dayton, OH; Phoenix, AZ; and Tacoma, WA. More than 250 of these discussions were with individuals who identified as white and working class, and they took place in neighborhood locations such as houses, community centers, diners, and places of worship. The detailed discussions enabled us to connect discussions between different communities and places in order to address some of the issues that we outlined at the start of this book.

The fieldwork took place in 2016 and 2017 during the course and aftermath of the 2016 presidential election, and after the inauguration of President Donald Trump. As a candidate, Trump stalked the discussions that we had with residents and stakeholders. He put himself forward as being the public voice of white working-class disenchantment on issues of immigration, change, and race—in short, pulling together anxieties over economic and cultural insecurity. Trump shaped the discussions but his message was met with a mixed response, with some people concurring while others strongly disagreed. This is a much more nuanced picture than put forward by commentators who viewed the ascent to the presidency as being underpinned by white working-class discontent.

This concluding chapter addresses the issues of defining white working-class communities, the challenges of choosing a president, the importance of qualitative data and lived experiences in revealing a granular and detailed understanding of macro-changes in society, and the prospects of cross-racial coalition building. This leads to implications for policy and practice as regards engaging with groups and communities who had been marginal to framing interventions prior to 2016.

In moving forward, it should be noted that the fieldwork took place in a specific moment in time of the 2016 presidential elections. The result was a political shock to many but should be seen in the context of wider global political change and the rise of populism. The success of Trump can be read across to the election of populist governments in Europe, Brazil, India, and the Philippines. Of course, the Brexit vote in 2016 by the UK to leave the EU was similarly viewed as a white working-class revolt against the elite under the campaign slogan of "Take Back Control," which overlaps with "Make America Great Again."

Looking ahead to the 2020 presidential elections and beyond, we question whether policymakers and researchers will learn from the messages of this research and others about the lived experiences of white working-class communities and their own sense of being left behind. As politics becomes even more febrile and society more fragmented, the only certainty is more uncertainty. Surely, this means that the importance of research such as that presented in this book is that it has a role to play in leading to a deeper understanding of experiences, as well as of the actions needed to develop and build political narratives that respond to the concerns of those who are part of the other America.

Defining the white working class

As we have discussed elsewhere in the book, "white" was largely silent throughout the discussions with participants across all the case-study sites. People mostly felt more comfortable using the term "working class" rather than "white working class" to describe and identify themselves. In short, this meant that they classed themselves and raced communities of color. Some of those we interviewed did not fully understand or could not admit that minority groups can also be both people of color and working class. This also played out in discussions about desirable neighborhoods and even cities, which became racialized. For example, in some instances, largely white neighborhoods were deemed as "good," with successful schools and low levels of crime, whereas minority areas were seen as being "bad," bracketing places with failing schools, high levels of violent crime, and general dysfunctionality.

When talking about the term "white working class," our participants tended to focus on the "working" of "white working class," with frequent references to the importance and value of hard work and how this brings in an income that enables an individual to become independent, having the ability to support immediate family as well as the wider community. Being in paid work and the benefits to the individual, family, and community that flowed could be cited as the glue that held together different people with different incomes and levels of education in an expansive view of what it means to be white and working class. Policymakers need to recognize the way in which values and how they are lived and experienced are important to this constituency. This may contribute to improving their understanding of white working-class communities.

Throughout our fieldwork, we were interested in hearing from residents as to how they defined and situated themselves as white working-class communities. As we have discussed elsewhere in the book, their views were markedly different from those deployed by policymakers.

Our discussions demonstrated the complexity of defining what it means to be white and working class in the US. In contrast to residents, who spoke at length about the importance of values, this was only marginal in discussions with key informants, who defaulted to focusing on college education, blue-collar jobs, and occasionally income thresholds. However, unlike residents, key informants were much more willing to highlight the "white" part of "white working class." This was overlooked by residents. Moreover, key informants were keen to bestow white privilege to working-class communities in relation to communities of color.

A key concern for us in this book is critically analyzing the meanings of "white working class" and specifically contrasting official definitions of white working-class communities with the lived experiences of people who identified as white and working class and participated in the research. The evidence demonstrated that the official account of emphasizing the importance of a college education, employment in "blue-collar" industries, and placing a ceiling threshold on income were at variance with the views of white working-class people. Instead, they spoke about economic insecurity irrespective of occupation and the lived experience of "living paycheck to paycheck." The term "working class" was articulated through a set of values and identities that was their lived experience and memory. These included working hard, reciprocity, and honesty, and they held sway across location, occupation, and income.

The implications of a political recalibration of the white working class have already been played out in the 2016 presidential election and the rise of Donald Trump from an outlier candidate to his ascent to the White House. As we look ahead and beyond the 2020 presidential campaign with an incumbent President Trump again trying to mobilize the votes of white working-class voters, much more work needs be done to achieve nuanced approaches to defining the white working class. At the very least, there is a need for both policymakers and academics to rethink their understanding of white working-class communities.

Selecting a president

The 2016 election intersected with our fieldwork and provided a backdrop to the discussions with white working-class communities across our case-study sites, both before and after the results were declared. In many respects, it could be put forward that the election was about hope and change, similar to the election of Barack Obama in 2008. As we have discussed, there are similarities between Obama and Trump as both were outsiders, led insurgent campaigns, and had a common establishment opponent, Hillary Clinton. It should be noted that there are considerable differences between Trump and Obama that have been played out during their respective terms of office. In 2016, Trump was about hope and change for white working-class people, and understanding that they felt ridiculed, silenced, and left behind in the context of making progress and nation building. The symbolism of Trump maximizing working-class anxieties in spaces such as a coalmine, donning a miner's helmet, or promising to keep the Carrier air conditioning factory open in Indianapolis rather than allowing it to relocate to Mexico was recognized and appealed to some participants in our research. In 2008 and during his second term, Obama appealed on hope and change to minority communities, middle-class and urban white voters, and millennials based on a rainbow coalition. Appeals to white working-class voters were muted.

The conventional view of white working-class voters mobilizing as a homogeneous group for Trump was not entirely borne out in our fieldwork. Many had reservations about his character and specifically his views of women, immigrants, and minority communities that prevented them from voting for him. Added to this, and going against the conventional narrative, there were examples of white working-class people who continued to support the Democrats locally. However, it is also true that there was a deep dislike of Hillary Clinton. Reflecting on the 2016 election and some of the themes that we discussed earlier in this concluding chapter, it was about who could best align themselves with perceived white working-class values and what it means to be working class. In this regard, it was clear that Trump tuned into these values of being honest, working hard, and being open, and highlighted white working-class concerns as part of a need to rebuild the economy while tapping into their experiences of cultural insecurity. This was achieved by references to the failures of NAFTA and globalization, as well as the threat from a range of groups constituting the "enemy within," from Muslims to Mexicans. In many ways, Clinton was an ideal opponent for Trump. She was perceived as part of the elite and establishment, and was disconnected from the experiences of white, working-class communities, as seen by her labeling of them as "deplorable."

Going forward to post-2020, we believe that politics needs to be organized differently, whether it is about Trump being successful in securing a second term in the White House or a Democratic victory. Our study showed that white working-class communities view themselves as being disconnected not just economically, but also politically. If political parties are serious about creating and sustaining winning political coalitions, they need to reach out to these voters and connect with their fears and concerns. In part, this means shifting beyond discussions between members of the elite in business, media, academia, and politics, relocating from "grasstops" to "grassroots," and listening to the lived experiences of working-class communities. Our participants in 2016, and indeed people around the world then and since, have limited or no trust in their political representatives; therefore, for traditional party-political organizations under pressure in many parts of the world, the success of the post-2020 and post-Trump politics could be based on those who seek to see people as neither Republicans nor Democrats, for example, but simply as voters. The blurring of political allegiances demands a paradigm shift to change the accumulated knowledge of political campaigning.

Looking ahead, successful national campaigns could, and should, be based on widening the much-celebrated "rainbow coalition" in a way that white working-class communities can be included as a critical component—no longer derided and ridiculed, but seen as being important as the US addresses the issues of race and class in the 21st century.

Cross-racial coalition building

There is a pressing need to be deliberative in cross-racial coalition building between white working-class communities and communities of color. Decades after the civil rights movement, there was very little in the way of examples of people coming together across racial boundaries. Many different reasons could be put forward for the lack of progress, including the way in which communities have been pitted against each other through the politics of suspicion and resentment.

Many stakeholders did not regard white working-class communities as being part of a progressive coalition; rather, they were viewed as a problematic group. However, for the most part, white working-class communities themselves wanted to engage with communities of color, although they did not have the know-how as to how this could be achieved. Overall, cross-racial coalition building was fleeting and "soft-wired" rather than sustained and "hard-wired." This opens up the prospect of foundations and policymakers creating opportunities to bring people together across racial and class divides, which will be even more challenging given the increasingly adversarial politics in the US since 2016. In this regard, innovation could be based on building grassroots coalitions between people, mediating discussions on sometimes difficult topics, and looking at the long-term sustainability of local communities working together to engage in local coalitions.

Documenting experiences

During the course of this book, we have emphasized the importance of documenting and analyzing the experiences of white working-class communities. Our fieldwork was based on 415 interviews across five different locations. More than 250 of these discussions were with residents in neighborhoods, often taking place in community centers, diners, and homes.

The significant reach and depth of the data demonstrate how people in different places and occupations connected with the concerns of this book, such as defining white working-class communities, the challenge of choosing a president, and creating opportunities to build coalitions of interest. We provided a focus group discussion between a group of residents just outside Phoenix, Arizona, that took place in January 2017 soon after the official inauguration of President Trump. The discussion provides the reader with an understanding of the themes that this book discusses, such as belonging, place, space, and change, which can be deployed as significant markers of how people locate themselves in relation to others. This in-depth case study underlined our findings in defining the white working class, where "white" was not explicit in discussions and the entire meaning of the term was contested. Similarly, there were contradictory views on race, with diverse neighborhoods associated with social problems and welfare needs. Donald Trump was seen as a different and unconventional candidate. In accord with the views of other residents interviewed across research sites, the new President was also seen as a polarizing figure, liked by some but despised by others. More importantly, the transcript highlighted how Trump's early policy interventions were viewed.

Implications for policy and practice

Redefining the white working class

One of the challenges of conducting research on white working-class communities is the shakiness of the definitions that are used, which are often devoid of lived experiences and nuance. The study revealed the limitations of current definitions of white working-class communities that emphasize income, occupation, or education. This is very narrow and does not reflect experiences and perceptions. People from white working-class communities did not understand the importance of a college degree as confirming that they had moved into the middle class, see the validity of "blue-collar" jobs at a time of austerity to legitimize working-class credentials, or agree upon a salary that denotes a working-class existence.

There was a gap between policy framing and grassroots experiences. Rather than continuing with narrow, administrative definitions, our research has highlighted that the white working class is seen as beyond income and education. There needs to be more nuanced approaches to defining the white working class that emphasizes the importance of common values, economic position, and stratification within the group. In this way, assumptions about the white working class that present it as a flat population that behaves in a stereotypical and predictable way, has conservative views on race and immigration, or defaults to voting for a certain political candidate may be challenged.

White working-class people need to be recognized as being as much a diverse grouping as any other in society, differing in terms of age, gender, sexual orientation, spatial location in terms of small or large city, and ethnic diversity within families and social networks. Expansive definitions and informed descriptions will increase opportunities to engage with people and organizations from a grouping that has been seen as parochial, closed, and defensive.

Bringing people together

The 2016 presidential campaign was one of the most divisive in US history. In this study, we witnessed the way in which national politics was played out locally in cities and neighborhoods. In our focus groups, some friends and families found themselves on opposing sides as divisions, both historical and contemporary, emerged in American society. People did not care for the way in which communities were set against each other and the assumed positions that were taken about different groups. The febrile atmosphere contributed to deepening the wells of suspicion and distrust. Many foundations work tirelessly to bridge these gaps by promoting greater levels of understanding between people and institutions, as well as between different communities in society. In this process, the voices of white working-class people need to be heard by institutions and other communities.

Civil society organizations can continue to hold political institutions to account, as De Tocqueville wanted, or increase the participation of people and trust toward politicians. To do this, they too perhaps need to reflect on how they intervene with white working-class communities and move toward a process of engagement based on active listening combined with challenge.

This study has demonstrated that white working-class people feel politically marginalized, culturally isolated, and economically vulnerable. As a consequence of their material position, talking about white privilege to working-class white people who are working two or three jobs to keep their families fed and a roof over their heads will be a difficult task. They point to other groups in society who have advocacy organizations, political patronage, and celebrity support, and see them speeding past them on the road to social mobility.

At the same time, and constituting a further challenge, is the use of racialized language, the denial of white privilege, and claims of reverse racism, all of which offend communities of color and ignore their lived experiences. The consequences of not doing anything could further deepen the crisis as the country moves to being even more diverse in the decades ahead. To build cross-racial coalitions requires trust and acknowledging who holds power.

Yet, the local, rather than the national or global, could provide the basis for community coalition building between the white working-class and communities of color. Given the reality of reduced federal spending on community development, together with a challenging political environment on issues of immigration and race, policymakers need to document and showcase good practice being implemented at the local and community levels. In our study, the examples are embryonic, but in each place, local people and organizations are attempting to find common ground between groups. In this way, an alternative prospectus may be generated on how white working-class communities are engaging in a positive way with communities of color rather than simply being viewed as their implacable adversaries.

Increasing organizational capacity

Many of the community activists and organizations who took part in the study were willing to build, consolidate, or create new coalitions of interest. However, they were limited in terms of their knowledge, and thus capability, to realize their ambitions. There is a need to increase organizational capacity and know-how, with special emphasis being placed on organizations and individuals who operate across boundaries, that is, those who have credibility and reach with white working-class communities but can also work with communities of color for common and mutual advantage. In each case-study site, we identified community activists who could become bridge builders and open up the prospect of new types of interventions in common areas of interest. In this way, future community organizers could be developed who reach across as well as reaching in, providing a blueprint to successfully negotiating the country of the future, rather than the past—to move from the other America to one America.

References

Alabama Opinion (2015) "What would Birmingham be without US Steel?" Available at: www.al.com/opinion/index.ssf/2015/04/what_would_birmingham_be_witho.html (accessed January 29, 2019).

Beider, H. (2015) *White working-class voices: Multiculturalism, community-building and change*. Bristol: Policy Press.

Beider, H., Harwood, S. and Chahal, K. (2017) *The other America: White-working class views on belonging, change, identity, and immigration*. Coventry: Coventry University.

Bonikowski, B. (2016) "Three lessons of contemporary populism in Europe and the United States." *The Brown Journal of World Affairs* 23(1): 9–24.

Bourke, B. (2014) "Positionality: Reflecting on the research process." *The Qualitative Report* 19(33): 1–9. Available at: https://nsuworks.nova.edu/tqr/vol19/iss33/ (accessed January 28, 2019).

Brownstein, R. (2011) "The white working class: The most pessimistic group in America." *The Atlantic*, May. Available at: www.theatlantic.com/politics/archive/2011/05/the-white-working-classthe-most-pessimistic-group-in-america/239584/ (accessed January 29, 2019).

CBS (Columbia Broadcasting System) (2016) "Hillary Clinton says half of Trump's supporters are in a 'basket of deplorables.'" *CBS News*, September 10.

Center for American Progress (2017) *What everyone should know about America's diverse working class*. Washington, DC: CAP.

Chahal, K. (1999) "Researching ethnicity: Experiences and concerns." In B. Broad (ed) *The politics of social work research and evaluation*. Birmingham: Venture Press.

Chotiner, I. (2017) "I'm hearing you're really angry." *Slate*, June 5. Available at: https://slate.com/news-and-politics/2017/06/advice-on-how-to-talk-to-the-white-working-class.html (accessed January 28, 2019).

CNBC (Consumer News and Business Channel) (2018) "Trump says 'the coal industry is back.' The government's jobs numbers say otherwise." Available at: www.cnbc.com/2018/08/23/trump-says-the-coal-industry-is-back-the-data-say-otherwise.html (accessed January 29, 2019).

Collins, M. (2005) *The likes of us: A biography of the white working class*. London: Granta.

Cramer, K.J. (2016) *The politics of resentment: Rural consciousness in Wisconsin and the rise of Scott Walker*. Chicago, IL: Chicago University Press.

De Tocqueville, A. (1838) *Democracy in America*. New York, NY: G. Dearborn & Co.

Donnan, S. (2016) "'Forgotten' white vote powers Trump to victory." *Financial Times*, November 9. Available at: www.ft.com/content/51534512-a648-11e6-8b69-02899e8bd9d1 (accessed January 26, 2019).

Dorning, M. (2016) "Trump's unthinkable victory is a tonic for disaffected Americans." *Bloomberg*, November 9. Available at: www.bloomberg.com/news/articles/2016-11-09/trump-s-unthinkable-victory-is-a-tonic-for-disaffected-americans (accessed January 28, 2019).

Dyer, R. (1997) *White*. London and New York, NY: Routledge.

Etherington, K. (2004) *Becoming a reflexive researcher: Using ourselves in research*. London: Jessica Kingsley Publishers.

Faber, D., Stephens, J., Wallis, V., Gottlieb, R., Levenstein, C., Coatar, P., and Boston Editorial Group of CNS (Cybercast News Services) (2017) "Trump's electoral triumph: Class, race, gender, and the hegemony of the polluter–industrial complex." *Capitalism Nature Socialism* 28(1): 1–15.

Fox, C. and Guglielmo, T. (2012) "Defining America's racial boundaries: Blacks, Mexicans, and European immigrants, 1890–1945." *American Journal of Sociology* 118(2): 327–79.

Frank, A.W. (1995) *The wounded storyteller: Body, illness and ethics*. Chicago, IL: University of Chicago Press.

Frank, T. (2004) *What's the matter with Kansas? How conservatives won the heart of America*. New York, NY: Henry Holt.

Freire, P. (2000) *Pedagogy of the oppressed* (30th anniversary edn). New York, NY: Continuum.

Galston, W. (2017) "The populist moment." *Journal of Democracy* 22(2): 21–33.

Garner, S. (2009) "Empirical research into white racialized identities in Britain." *Sociology Compass* 3(5): 789–802.

Gest, J. (2016) *The new minority: White working class politics in an age of immigration and inequality*. New York, NY: Oxford University Press.

Glasser, S. and Rush, G. (2016) "What's going on with America's white people?" *Politico*, September/October. Available at: www.politico.com/magazine/story/2016/09/problems-white-people-america-society-class-race-214227 (accessed January 29, 2019).

Greenberg, S. (2014) "The battle for working people begins with government reform." In The Democratic Strategist (ed) *Second roundtable on the white working class*. Available at: www.thedemocraticstrategist.org/_memos/tds_WWC_roundtable_two_final.pdf (accessed June 20, 2017).

Greven, T. (2016) *The rise of right-wing populism in Europe and the United States: A comparative perspective*. Berlin: Friedrich-Ebert-Stiftung.

Gridron, N. and Bonikowski, B. (2014) *Varieties of populism: Literature review and research agenda*. Weatherhead Working Paper Series, No. 13-0004. Cambridge: Harvard University Press.

Hartigan, J. (1999) *Racial situations: Class predicaments of whiteness in Detroit*. Princeton, NJ: Princeton University Press.

Hochschild, A. (2016) *Strangers in their own land: Anger and mourning on the American right*. New York, NY: The New Press.

Huntington, S. (1997) *The clash of civilizations and the remaking of world order*. New York, NY: Touchstone.

Isenberg, N. (2016) *White trash: The 400-year untold history of class in America*. New York, NY: Viking.

Jacobs, B. (2016) "Hillary Clinton regrets 'basket of deplorables' remark as Trump attacks." *The Guardian*, September 11. Available at: www.theguardian.com/us-news/2016/sep/10/hillary-clinton-basket-of-deplorables-donald-trump (accessed January 29, 2019).

Jacobson, M. (1998) *Whiteness of a different color: European immigrants and the alchemy of race*. Cambridge: Harvard University Press.

Jardina, A. (2019) *White identity politics*. Cambridge: Cambridge University Press.

Kazin, M. (1995) *The populist persuasion: An American history*. Ithaca, NY: Cornell University Press.

Kefalas, M. (2003) *Working-class heroes: Protecting home, community, and nation in a Chicago neighborhood*. Berkeley, CA: University of California Press.

Kerstetter, K. (2012) "Insider, outsider, or somewhere in between: The impact of researchers' identities on the community-based research process." *Journal of Rural Social Science* 27(2): 99–117.

Kozlowski, M. and Perkins, H.A. (2016) "Environmental justice in Appalachia Ohio? An expanded consideration of privilege and the role it plays in defending the contaminated status quo in a white, working-class community." *Local Environment: The International Journal of Justice and Sustainability* 21(10): 1288–304.

Kunzru, H. (2016) "Hillbilly Elegy by JD Vance review—Does this memoir really explain Trump's victory?" *The Guardian*, December 7. Available at: www.theguardian.com/books/2016/dec/07/hillbilly-elegy-by-jd-vance-review (accessed January 27, 2019).

Lamont, M., Park, B., and Ayala-Hurtado, E. (2017) "Trump's electoral speeches and his appeal to the American white working class." *The British Journal of Sociology* 68(1): 153-180.

Levison, A. (2013) *The white working class today: Who they are, what they think and how progressives can regain their support*. Washington, DC: Democratic Strategist Press.

Linkon, S. and Russo, J. (2002) *Steeltown U.S.A.: Work and memory in Youngstown*. Lawrence, KS: University of Kansas Press.

Maisano, C. (2017) "The new culture of poverty." *Catalyst* 1(2). Available at: https://catalyst-journal.com/vol1/no2/new-culture-of-poverty-maisano (accessed January 29, 2019).

Marusza, J. (1997) "Urban white working class males and the possibilities of collective anger: Patrolling Riley Road." *The Urban Review* 29(2): 97–112.

McDermott, M. (2006) *Working-class white: The making and unmaking of race relations*. Berkeley, CA: University of California Press.

McDermott, M. and Samson, F. (2005) "White racial and ethnic identity in the United States." *Annual Review of Sociology* 31: 245–61.

McElwee, S. and McDaniel, J. (2017) "Economic anxiety didn't make people vote Trump, racism did." *The Nation*, May 8. Available at: www.thenation.com/article/economic-anxiety-didnt-make-people-vote-trump-racism-did/ (accessed January 29, 2019).

Moerman, M. (1974) "Accomplishing ethnicity." In R. Turner (ed) *Ethnomethodology*. Harmondsworth: Penguin, pp 54–68.

Mudde, C. (2007) *Populist radical right parties in Europe*. Cambridge: Cambridge University Press.

Murray, C. (2012) *Coming apart: The state of white America, 1960–2010*. New York, NY: Crown Forum.

New York Times (2016) "Why Trump won: Working-class whites." Available at: www.nytimes.com/2016/11/10/upshot/why-trump-won-working-class-whites.html (accessed January 28, 2019).

New York Times (2018) "At Carrier, the factory that Trump saved, morale is through the floor." Available at: www.nytimes.com/2018/08/10/business/economy/carrier-trump-absenteeism-morale.html (accessed January 29, 2019).

Opportunity America, American Enterprise Institute, and Brookings (2018) *Work, skills, community: Restoring opportunity for the working class*. Washington, DC: Opportunity America, AEI, and Brookings.

OSF (Open Society Foundations) (2014) *Building bridges: London Borough of Waltham Forest*. New York, NY: Open Society Foundations.

Patton, M.Q. (2002) *Qualitative research & evaluation methods* (3rd edn). Thousand Oaks, CA: Sage Publications.

Pierce, S., Bolter, J. and Selee, A. (2018) *U.S. immigration policy under Trump: Deep changes and lasting impacts*. New York, NY: Migration Policy Institute.

PRRI (Public Research Religion Institute) (2012) *Beyond guns and god: Understanding the complexities of the white working class in America*. Washington, DC: Public Research Religion Institute.

PRRI (2017) *Beyond economics: Fears of cultural displacement pushed the white working class to Trump*. Washington, DC: Public Research Religion Institute.

Pruitt, L. (2016) "Welfare queens and white trash." *Southern California Interdisciplinary Law Journal* 25 ("Reframing the Welfare Queen" Symposium): 289.

Putnam, R. (2000) *Bowling alone: The collapse and revival of American community*. New York, NY: Simon & Schuster.

Qin, D. (2016) "Positionality." In N. Naples, C.R. Hoogland, M. Wickramasinghe, and W.C.A. Wong (eds) *The Wiley Blackwell encyclopedia of gender and sexuality studies*. Hoboken, NJ: John Wiley and Sons Ltd.

Rieder, J. (1985) *Canarsie: The Jews and Italians of Brooklyn against liberalism*. Cambridge: Harvard University Press.

Roediger, D. (2005) *Working toward whiteness: How America's immigrant's became white: The strange journey from Ellis Island to the suburbs*. New York, NY: Basic Books.

Sasson, E. (2016) "Blame Trump's victory on college-educated whites, not the working class." *The New Republic*. Available at: https://newrepublic.com/article/138754/blame-trumps-victory-college-educated-whites-not-working-class (accessed January 27, 2019).

Silver, N. (2016) "The mythology of Trump's 'working class' support." Available at: https://fivethirtyeight.com/features/the-mythology-of-trumps-working-class-support/ (accessed January 29, 2019).

Standing, G. (2011) *The precariat: The new dangerous class*. London: Bloomsbury.

Stoddart, K. (2002) "Researching white racial identity." *The American Behavioural Scientist* 45(8): 1254–1264.

Teixeira, R. and Abramowitz, A. (2008) *The decline of the white working class and the rise of a mass upper middle class*. Washington, DC: Brookings.

The Atlantic (2018) "The Democrats' white-people problem." Available at: www.theatlantic.com/magazine/archive/2018/12/the-democrats-white-people-problem/573901/ (accessed January 29, 2019).

The Guardian (2016) "How Donald Trump seduced America's white working class." Available at: www.theguardian.com/commentisfree/2016/sep/10/jd-vance-hillbilly-elegy-donald-trump-us-white-poor-working-class (accessed January 29, 2019).

Vance, J.D. (2016) *Hillbilly elegy: A memoir of a family and culture in crisis*. New York, NY: Harper Collins.

Vanity Fair (2017) "Inside how Trump won the white working class." Available at: www.vanityfair.com/news/2017/01/how-trump-won-the-white-working-class (accessed January 29, 2019).

Walsh, J. (2014) *What's the matter with white people: Finding our way in the next America*. New York, NY: Touchstone Books.

Wellman, D.T. (1977) *Portraits of white racism*. Cambridge: Cambridge University Press.

Williams, J. (2017) "We need to redefine what working class means." *Time Magazine*. Available at www.time.com/4899906/donald-trump-white-working-class/ (accessed January 29, 2019).

Wray, M. (2006) *Not quite white: White trash and the boundaries of whiteness*. Durham, NC: Duke University Press.

Yancy, G. (2008) *Black bodies, white gazes: The continuing significance of race*. Lanham, MD: Rowman and Littlefield.

Appendices

All appendices are reproduced from Beider et al (2017).

Appendix A: Focus groups demographics

	Bay Ridge	Birmingham	Dayton	Phoenix	Tacoma	Total
Gender						
Men	15	10	12	5	24	45.8%
Women	13	22	15	22	6	54.2%
Age						
Young adults (18–44)	7	16	19	16	16	51.4%
Middle-aged adults (45–65)	6	15	7	7	6	28.5%
Mature adults (65+)	15	1	1	4	8	20.1%
Total	**28**	**32**	**27**	**27**	**30**	**144**

Appendix B: 2016 presidential election results by county and state for study sites

	Bay Ridge	Birmingham	Dayton	Phoenix	Tacoma
County	***King***	***Jefferson***	***Montgomery***	***Maricopa***	***Pierce***
Trump	17.8%	52.2%	48.4%	49.1%	42.1%
Clinton	79.3%	45.0%	47.1%	45.7%	49.5%
State	***NY***	***AL***	***OH***	***AZ***	***WA***
Trump	37.5%	62.9%	52.1%	49.5%	38.1%
Clinton	58.8%	34.6%	43.5%	45.4%	54.3%

Source: CNN Election Results 2016 (available at: http://edition.cnn.com/election/results)

Appendix C: Regional perspective: race and ethnic profile

	Bay Ridge	Birmingham	Dayton	Phoenix	Tacoma
	Brooklyn–King County	*Birmingham–Hoover MSA*[a]	*Dayton MSA*	*Phoenix–Mesa–Scottsdale MSA*	*Seattle–Tacoma–Bellevue MSA*
Total population	2,595,259	1,138,476	801,472	4,407,915	3,614,361
White	36%	64%	77%	57%	66%
Latino	20%	4%	2%	30%	9%
Asian	11%	1%	2%	4%	13%
Black	31%	28%	15%	5%	5%
Other	2%	2%	3%	4%	6%
Total	100%	100%	100%	100%	100%

Note: [a] MSA = Metropolitan Statistical Area.

Source: 2011–15 American Community Survey

Appendix D: Local perspective: race and ethnic profile

	Bay Ridge	Birmingham	Dayton	Phoenix	Tacoma
Total population	81,906	212,211	141,368	1,514,208	203,481
White	64%	22%	52%	45%	60%
Latino	18%	4%	4%	41%	11%
Asian	15%	1%	1%	4%	10%
Black	2%	72%	40%	7%	10%
Other	2%	1%	3%	4%	9%
Total	100%	100%	100%	100%	100%

Source: 2011–15 American Community Survey

Appendix E: Regional perspective: foreign-born population

	Bay Ridge	Birmingham	Dayton	Phoenix	Tacoma
	Brooklyn–King County	*Birmingham–Hoover MSA*[a]	*Dayton MSA*	*Phoenix–Mesa–Scottsdale MSA*	*Seattle–Tacoma–Bellevue MSA*
Total foreign-born (% of total population)	972,294 (38%)	45,191 (4%)	31,684 (4%)	634,777 (14%)	623,751 (17%)
% naturalised	57%	32%	48%	37%	50%
% not a US citizen	43%	68%	52%	63%	50%
Total	100%	100%	100%	100%	100%

Note: [a] MSA = Metropolitan Statistical Area.

Source: 2011–15 American Community Survey

Appendix F: Local perspective: foreign-born population

	Bay Ridge	Birmingham	Dayton	Phoenix	Tacoma
Total foreign-born (% of total population)	28,897 (35%)	7,604 (4%)	6,184 (4.4%)	303,364 (20%)	27,513 (14%)
% naturalized	63%	26%	37%	30%	53%
% not a US citizen	37%	74%	63%	70%	47%
Total	100%	100%	100%	100%	100%

Source: 2011–15 American Community Survey

Appendix G: Regional perspective: demographics of white, non-Hispanic population

	Bay Ridge	Birmingham	Dayton	Phoenix	Tacoma
	Brooklyn–King County	*Birmingham–Hoover MSA*[a]	*Dayton MSA*	*Phoenix–Mesa–Scottsdale MSA*	*Seattle–Tacoma–Bellevue MSA*
Total population	2,595,259	1,138,476	801,472	4,407,915	3,614,361
White	36%	64%	77%	57%	66%
Poverty	23%	11%	13%	10%	8%
Unemployed (16 years or older in labor force)	7%	78%	7%	7%	6%
Owner-occupied housing unit (with white householder)	36%	7%	69%	69%	65%
High School diploma or less (25 years or older)	31%	39%	39%	28%	25%

Note: [a] MSA = Metropolitan Statistical Area.

Source: 2011–15 American Community Survey

Appendix H: Local perspective: demographics of white, non-Hispanic population

	Bay Ridge	Birmingham	Dayton	Phoenix	Tacoma
Total population	81,906	212,211	141,368	1,514,208	203,481
White	64%	22%	52%	45%	60%
Poverty	14%	20%	26%	12%	14%
Unemployed (16 years or older in labor force)	9%	7%	11%	7%	8%
Owner-occupied housing unit (with white householder)	39%	52%	55%	63%	55%
High School diploma or less (25 years or older)	30%	27%	46%	28%	35%

Source: 2011–15 American Community Survey

Index

M

N

O

P